T.W. Schultz
1970

Water Transfers:

Economic Efficiency

and

Alternative Institutions

WATER TRANSFERS: ECONOMIC EFFICIENCY AND ALTERNATIVE INSTITUTIONS

by

L. M. Hartman and Don Seastone

Published for Resources for the Future, Inc.

By The Johns Hopkins Press, Baltimore and London

RESOURCES FOR THE FUTURE, INC.
1755 Massachusetts Avenue, N.W., Washington, D.C. 20036

Resources for the Future is a nonprofit corporation for research and education in the development, conservation, and use of natural resources and the improvement of the quality of the environment. It was established in 1952 with the cooperation of the Ford Foundation. Part of the work of Resources for the Future is carried out by its resident staff; part is supported by grants to universities and other nonprofit organizations. Unless otherwise stated, interpretations and conclusions in RFF publications are those of the authors; the organization takes responsibility for the selection of significant subjects for study, the competence of the researchers, and their freedom of inquiry.

This book is one of RFF's studies in water resources, which are directed by Charles W. Howe. The research was supported by a grant to Colorado State University, where L. M. Hartman is professor of economics. Don Seastone, formerly with Colorado State University, is now professor of economics at the University of Calgary, Canada. The manuscript was edited by Roma K. McNickle. The charts were drawn by Frank and Clare Ford. The index was prepared by Rachel Johnson.

RFF editors: Henry Jarrett, Vera W. Dodds, Nora E. Roots, Tadd Fisher.

Foreword

Water is a critical factor in the continued prosperity and growth of the western United States. While water has not constituted a constraint on the growth of the West to date, whether or not it will in the future depends upon public policy and expenditure decisions and upon the economic efficiency of the market mechanism in directing available water supplies to the uses of highest social value.

Two facts about the West are clear: (1) significant additional supplies of water will be quite costly; (2) present supplies are not used as efficiently as they could be. These two facts suggest that more efficient use of existing supplies, in the senses of more careful application in present uses and shifts toward higher-valued uses, may be at least a partial substitute for new supplies.

It is thus of interest to determine the relative efficiencies of different types of market processes through which water rights are transferred from one use to another. The institutional setting constituting the legal and organizational framework within which transfers are negotiated in large part determines the nature of the transfer process. It is to the analysis of the comparative economic efficiencies of alternative institutional arrangements for the transfer of water rights that the authors turn in this volume. A great deal of attention is directed toward external impacts of transfers, especially return flows and income changes in other sectors, and their effect on the economic efficiency of market transfers.

This volume is a part of a long-standing program of water resource studies at Resources for the Future which has increasingly turned attention toward the analysis of alternative institutional arrangements for the management and development of water resources. Published results of other recent related work include *Northern California's Water Industry: The Comparative Efficiency of Public Enterprise in Developing a Scarce Natural Resource,* by Joe S. Bain, Richard E. Caves, and Julius Margolis (1966); *The ORSANCO Story,* by Edward J. Cleary (1967); *Managing*

Water Quality: Economics, Technology, Institutions, by Allen V. Kneese and Blair T. Bower (1968); and *Water Management Innovations in England,* by Lyle E. Craine (1969). Work closely related to that of Hartman and Seastone concerning western water problems is continuing at Resources for the Future.

September, 1969   CHARLES W. HOWE
                                           Director, Water Resources Program

Authors' Acknowledgments

This book grew out of a study entitled "The Social Mechanism of the Rural-Urban Water Transfer," which was conducted by the authors in the Department of Economics at Colorado State University. The study was supported by a grant from Resources for the Future. The authors wish to acknowledge their appreciation to RFF for its generous help throughout the study. The outputs from that study are not represented entirely by this book, since many externalities accrued to the authors, the department, and the university as the study progressed.

We acknowledge an intellectual debt to members of RFF and to our colleagues in the university, particularly to John Krutilla, Irving Fox (now at the University of Wisconsin), Allen Kneese, and Charles Howe of RFF; and to Rufus Hughes, Stephen Smith, David Seckler and Paul Barkley of the Department of Economics at C.S.U. The extent of this debt is hard to assess because it is difficult for a writer to keep separate the ideas that develop from solitary thinking and those that are borrowed or develop as a combined product of several minds. The original conception of the study was developed within the staff of RFF and crystallized in correspondence with the authors. The main outline of the ideas presented in the book represents further development and expansion of the original plans.

We wish to acknowledge the help of graduate assistants Barry Asumas and Lee Grey in collecting the information presented in chapters IV, V, and VI. David Holland and Edward Lundgren contributed to the development of the empirical analysis presented in chapter VIII.

Several of the chapters in the book have appeared as articles. Chapter II was published in *Water Resources Research,* volume I, number II, 1965. Chapter III was revised from an article appearing in *Land Economics,* volume XXXIX, February 1963, entitled "Alternative Institutions for Water Transfer: The Experience in Colorado and New Mexico." Part of chapter VII was given as a paper at a Western

Resources Conference and appeared as a chapter in RFF's *Water Research,* edited by Allen V. Kneese and Stephen C. Smith (1966).

Finally, we wish to thank Charles Howe for his patient and helpful editorial assistance in the final stages of manuscript review, contributing both to subject matter development and language. We also wish to thank Roma K. McNickle, who edited the manuscript. Her editorial experience and understanding of western water problems were a happy combination.

CONTENTS

LIST OF TABLES

Appendixes

LIST OF FIGURES

Water Transfers:

Economic Efficiency

and

Alternative Institutions

CHAPTER I

INTRODUCTION

Problems associated with the ownership and management of water resources have existed in the arid western United States since the early days of settlement. The problems have become more serious as population and economic activity have increased; indeed it has become recognized that water could be the resource which will ultimately limit the region's growth. One possible and, to date, important way of preventing this resource from becoming a limit to regional growth is to permit the transfer of water from low-valued to higher-valued uses. Such reallocations generally involve a transfer of ownership rights and a physical transfer of the flow.

The basic question to which this book is addressed is: To what extent do existing organizational arrangements for the management of the water resource permit reallocations to take place efficiently? The transfer arrangements analyzed consist of the market possibilities for water transfers which exist under different legal systems and within various prominent types of water organizations.

WATER TRANSFERS AND THE PRIVATE MARKET SYSTEM

The concept of water as an economic resource is gradually emerging as water becomes more scarce in relation to demand. In a developing economic system, it is important that any resource be mobile in order to facilitate changes in use, and this gives rise to the water transfer problem. Devising property-right rules and organizational facilities to permit market transfers of water is a part of the evolution of water as an economic resource. Physical interdependencies of water users preclude simple property-right systems such as exist for most productive assets.

Economic development pressures upon water use offer an impetus for bypassing the private market system for water transfers because of the ubiquity of impacts on third parties, nonmarket values attached to water use, and the magnitude of investment which is often needed to effect

1

transfers.[1] A free market system in water would not take into account third-party effects and nonmarket factors. To this extent, it must be augmented or replaced by new extra-market organizations.

EXTERNALITIES

The importance of the effects of water transfers on persons who are not direct parties to the market transaction warrants special mention of the concept of externalities (sometimes termed third-party effects or spillover effects).

A conception of externalities as a basis for political theory was expressed by John Dewey several decades ago.[2] In an exposition of the logical grounds for public action, Dewey pointed out that if we observe the actions of individuals performed for specific reasons, we find that the actions have effects upon individuals other than those immediately involved. From this, he stated:

> . . . we are led to remark that the consequences are of two kinds, those which affect the persons directly engaged in a transaction, and those which affect others beyond those immediately concerned. In this distinction we find the germ of the distinction between the private and the public. When indirect consequences are recognized and there is an effort to regulate them, something having the traits of a state comes into existence.

In the literature of economics,[3] an externality occurs when the action of an individual or group of individuals has economic consequences which are not priced by the market. Then the market process does not perform the function of causing the individual whose action results in an externality to adjust his behavior in accord with the consequences. In terms of welfare, the existence of externalities reduces the optimizing tendencies of the market for allocating resources because there is not an accurate feedback of incentive rewards or penalties to control the producer of the effect.

In the natural resources field generally, the problem of externalities is widespread, and various organizational arrangements and regulatory measures have been adopted or proposed to cope with it.[4] Laws have been written and established by the courts to protect the third parties in

---

[1] John V. Krutilla and Otto Eckstein, *Multiple Purpose River Development* (Johns Hopkins Press for Resources for the Future, 1958).

[2] John Dewey, *The Public and Its Problems* (The Swallow Press, Inc.), p. 12.

[3] See Sherman Krupp, "Analytic Economics and the Logic of External Effects," *American Economic Review,* May 1963; and E. J. Mishan, *Welfare Economics* (Random House, 1964).

[4] See, for example, Roland McKean, *Efficiency in Government through Systems Analysis* (Wiley, 1958); and S. V. Ciriacy-Wantrup, *Resource Conservation Economics and Policies* (University of California Press, 1952).

water transfers. Special districts have been formed to internalize some of the externalities. The general tendency in institutional development has been to modify market procedures or completely replace them.

Thus, particularly with respect to water use, economic development involves not only development of the resource and related capital facilities but also institutional development. Changing the form of organizations is a fundamental part of economic growth, for the correlates of growth involve an increasing complexity of relations among economic agents.[5] Institutional development for water use has proceeded to an advanced stage in some geographic areas. In other areas, use and development are still performed primarily within the traditional property-right market-system rules. The state of institutional development appears to be highly correlated with the stage of economic development and population and, consequently, with the relative scarcity of the resource. Economic development and population growth tend to result in a predominantly urban culture with different values than those of a rural culture, which tends to be more traditionally oriented. In the industrial sector, progress in the form of technological innovations and capital growth has been facilitated by widespread organizational innovations.[6]

EVALUATION CRITERIA FOR ORGANIZATIONS

Evaluation of an institutional system requires measurement of the degree to which the system performs functions in accord with community goals. One function of an economic system is the allocation of resources. A test of the performance of this function is the well-known economic efficiency criterion which corresponds roughly to the maximization of national income.[7] A necessary condition for an efficient allocation of a resource is that the value of the marginal product of the resource be equal in all uses. If this condition holds, income from the resource cannot be increased by any reallocation. Under special circumstances a free-market allocation will approach this condition. Study of the free-market price system has revealed certain principles of organization which are the basis for its success. These principles concern the information and control aspects of the system.[8] The unique and amazing aspect of the price-

[5] Max Weber, *The Theory of Social and Economic Organization,* trans. A. M. Henderson and Talcott Parsons (Oxford University Press, 1947).

[6] See, for example, John Kenneth Galbraith, *The New Industrial State* (Houghton Mifflin, 1967).

[7] The economic efficiency measure is more inclusive than national income, for it would take into account any values measurable in money terms whether or not they were registered in market transactions; e.g., the value of "free" publicly provided recreation.

[8] See Friedrich Hayek, "The Price System as a Mechanism for Using Knowl-

market system, from an organizational point of view and in view of these interdependencies, is the relative autonomy of all the behavioral units in the system and the amount of information transmission and control exercised by the price mechanism.

All exchange transactions—a commodity purchase or a use and payment for factor inputs—involve reciprocal control. In the purchase of a water right the economic simplicity of this relationship of buyer to seller becomes complicated because the resource to which the owner is selling the right is interrelated in supply with the rights of others. Hence simple reciprocity does not hold between buyer and seller. It appears that at least three different but related approaches to coping with the problem have been tried in management of water resources. These are: (1) modification of traditional property-right procedures; (2) formation of collectivities of holding rights; and (3) centralized control, as is the case with the Tennessee Valley Authority. Water use in the West has proceeded on the basis of (1) and (2).

In this study there are, therefore, two basic types of institutions to analyze in terms of the efficiency of their allocative function: the law and its implementing procedures; and the rules governing the internal and external operation of various kinds of collectivities.

One can suppose that societies choose, not necessarily in a literal sense, particular techniques from a set and that that choice is not aimless. Several constraints operate to limit the choice—the specific problem which they perceive, past experience, some scale of values, and perhaps some apparently random elements too. A judge may decide a case on a new principle of law, setting a precedent for subsequent similar cases. An interest group may press through new legislation. Community leaders may organize opinion for local action. Some such processes were involved in bringing into existence the organizations and legal systems discussed in this book, but no attempt is made to explain the process or to recommend how suggested changes might be implemented. One essential ingredient for rational social action is an understanding of the performance of existing systems and of the likely consequences of changing them. This study is viewed as a contribution to that kind of knowledge.

PLAN OF THE BOOK

The process of understanding the problems stemming from water transfers would most expeditiously proceed in the order of physical, economic,

---

edge," in *Comparative Economic Systems,* Morris Berstein, ed. (Richard Irwin, 1965).

and then institutional considerations. Normative recommendations for improved efficiency would, at the present stage of water-related technology and knowledge, most likely concern the institutional setting. The basic problem is here viewed as an adjustment of water-resource institutions to a changing economic environment with physical processes as given constraints. The study developed around the analysis of externalities and water law. The typical organizations of the ditch company and the water conservancy district were brought into the study, since the form of water-right ownership embodied in these organizations is predominant for irrigation use.

The physical externality that appears to be most universally present in transfers of water between locations or types of uses is that due to return flow or, more specifically, to the relation between diversion and consumptive use. In the literature of welfare economics, this type of effect is referred to as a technological externality and is applied to effects on the supply of resources to third parties resulting from a market transaction. Chapter II analyzes the implications of this type of effect on the conditions required for efficient transfers of water and relates this analysis to existing appropriation law on property rights in water.

Chapter III presents a comparative analysis of the performance of two legal systems for regulating transfers between water users: the Colorado and New Mexico systems. The comparison focuses on the use of information and the creation of uncertainty. Chapters IV, V, and VI report on typical organizational forms: the ditch company and two different water conservancy districts. The emphasis is upon their handling of transfers *within* the organization, as distinguished from state water law systems which regulate transfers *between* organizations.

The transfer of water between uses or locations of use does change the economic base of communities, and the extent of the income effect from this type of change depends upon resource mobility, economies of scale, and so forth. A theoretical discussion of the income interdependency effect is presented in chapter VII, and some estimates are presented in chapter VIII. These materials were placed last because of their importance in current interstate transfer controversies and their obvious political relevance. The reader may choose to concentrate on the externality effects by reading chapters II, VII, and VIII, and then refer to the legal and organizational systems in chapters III, IV, V, and VI.

CHAPTER II

EFFICIENCY CRITERIA FOR MARKET TRANSFERS OF WATER

This chapter considers the allocation of water within a single basin from an atomistic decision-making point of view. Management models have been developed by others for stochastic storage-flow relationships; management of ground and surface supplies; and coordination of various uses such as power generation, flood protection, municipal, and irrigation demands in dynamic sequential-decision models.[1] The point of view taken in these studies has been to assume implicitly a centrally controlled system with an income maximization objective. We are considering a system composed of many independent users who hold property rights to water in a situation where there are economic forces for reallocation. The question to be investigated concerns the legal procedures for transfer of ownership rights and how these procedures operate in an efficiency sense. The motivation for this problem grows out of consideration of the rural-urban transfer and the efficacy of the market in performing this allocative function.

The allocation of annual river flow involves three aspects in terms of property-right specification—allocation to use, to space location, and to a time designation. The Colorado appropriation doctrine consists of a priority system for deciding who gets the water during certain seasons of the year. Use and location are specified at the time a right is established. The chapter considers the transfer of a water right between locations and uses and makes an economic evaluation of procedures under the Colorado doctrine, using simplifying assumptions concerned with return flow lags and variability of flow.

PROPERTY RIGHTS AND PHYSICAL SUPPLY

Once a pattern of use has been established in a river basin and the waters are fully appropriated along the stream, any change in use or

[1] See, for example, Ali Eshett and M. W. Bittinger, "Stream-Aquifer System Analysis for Conjunctive-Use Operations" (paper presented at American Society of Civil Engineers Hydraulics Division Conference, Vicksburg, Mississippi, 1964).

point of diversion may alter the quantity and quality of water supply available to other users. This change may be critical and cause actual damage to other rights only during low-flow years or seasons. However, damage is potentially inherent in any change in the established pattern of use. Assessment of the effect of a change represents the crux of the problem of physical interrelationships and provides necessary data for an exchange of an ownership right to water.

Two institutional procedures, with considerable variation from state to state, are currently used to protect third parties to a transfer negotiation. In some states transfer proceedings are handled by district courts, whereas in other states proceedings are handled by an administrative agency.[2] In either case the purchaser petitions for permission to change the point of diversion and/or the use of a water right. If other water users on the stream protest, he must provide evidence that the transfer will cause no damage or—if it does—assess the probable extent of such damage. On the basis of the evidence presented, precedent cases, and/or statutory law, the court or the administrative agency then rules on whether a transfer will be permitted and the amount of water to be transferred.

The water uses considered in this study are off-stream uses (irrigation, municipal, and industrial uses), where the transfer is most likely to be from irrigation to municipal and industrial uses. For off-stream uses only part of the water diverted from a stream is used consumptively; that is, in a way that makes water unavailable for further use. For example, in a stream where pollution is critical, addition of further pollutants represents consumptive use to the extent of additional water required in the stream to dilute the pollutants to a tolerable level.

For municipalities and industry, nonconsumptively used water is returned directly to the stream, where it is readily available for re-use, at least for some purposes. In irrigation, nonconsumptively used water may either flow directly back to the stream or percolate into the underground, from which it either flows back to the stream or is available for pumping from the aquifer. Thus, return flows from one diversion are available for re-use and become a source of supply for junior water rights; i.e., those rights granted at later dates and thus having lower priority. The junior rights are dependent on these return flows only during low-flow periods; but since such periods may be critical, owners of junior rights will oppose any change in use from senior rights that affect return flows. Also, change in use may affect the quality as well as the quantity of return flow, creating another aspect of transfers of ownership and changing use that may alter available supply where quality is an impor-

2 See chapter III.

tant consideration. Thus, it becomes apparent that a property right to water, which is a use right, must be defined in terms of the effect a use has on supply available to other users. The quantity of water for diversion under any given right is therefore dependent on the place and type of use.

EXTERNAL EFFECTS AND EFFICIENCY CRITERIA

The following analysis considers the problem resulting from an exchange of property rights where private interests seek to maximize private economic gain. Measurement of use is for a long-period average restricted to certain seasons of the year, as it is determined by the courts in the rights transfer procedure. The traditional equilibrium test of an efficient allocation of resources is that the value of the marginal product from the resource be equal in all uses. In water use one may consider either a stock measurement such as an acre-foot or a flow such as cubic feet per second, where the flow is available for a certain period depending on priority ranking and availability. Value per unit of water resource can be considered on an annual basis for conceptual analysis, although in exchange of rights the value will be a capital value.

The relevant measurement of use in a productive process, or for domestic use, is the reduction in available supply incurred from the use, termed consumptive use. Consumptive use thus becomes one of the most important factors for computing the value of the marginal product in determining allocation efficiency. However, availability of return flow depends on location of use on the stream, so that location with respect to re-use potential of return flow also becomes part of the question of efficiency. In general, upstream use will be favored over downstream use because of the re-use potential of return flow. For example, the return flow of the last user near the mouth of the stream has no re-use; thus consumptive use, for all practical purposes, would be equivalent to the amount diverted from the stream. Also, where water is transferred long distances, as by ditch or unlined canal, losses occur through evaporation and seepage, so that the point of measurement, for valuing water use, should be at the point of diversion, not at the point of use. With these ideas in mind, consideration can be given to the question of efficiency.

Suppose there are n different diversions on a given stretch of river for various uses, such as municipal, industrial, and agricultural. If we designate by R_i the fraction returned to the stream from the ith diversion ($0 \leq R_i \leq 1$) and if we denote by S_1 the farthest upstream diversion measured in cubic feet per second flow, then the feasible total productive use of the amount S_1 would be $S_1 + R_1 S_1 + R_2 R_1 S_1 + R_3 R_2 R_1 S_1 \ldots + R_{n-1} R_{n-2} \ldots R_1 S_1$. (We are here following the convention that ordering of subscripts indicates the relative location on the stream.) Each term represents a potential quantity of water for use; i.e., S_1 is the original amount diverted, R_1S_1 is returned, and again at the second diversion $R_2R_1S_1$ is returned and so forth to the nth diversion.

If $R_1 = R_2 \ldots = R_n$, the above series is geometric and the sum is $S_1[1/(1 - R) - R^n/(1 - R)]$ or approximately $S_1/(1 - R)$, if n is large. Thus, $1/(1 - R)$, which may be considered as multiplier of S_1, approximates the total use of the diversion S_1 and is an upper limit on total use. A value of $R = 0.5$ gives a multiplier of 2, indicating that an initial supply will be approximately doubled through re-use if one-half of each amount diverted is returned to the stream or to an underground aquifer for pumping, and there are many uses on the stream.

If we denote the value of the marginal product of a unit of diverted water as f'_i, then the total marginal value of a unit diverted at the ith point is $f'_i + f'_{i+1}R_i + f'_{i+2}R_iR_{i+1}. \ldots$ Location on the stream becomes relevant only when the downstream uses are not sufficient to exhaust the re-use potential of the return flow and/or when the marginal value of these uses is different. For example, if there were only two uses on a stream, the marginal value of the upstream use would include the value of the marginal product in the initial use plus return flow use, $f'_1 + f'_2R_1$; marginal value for the downstream use would only be f'_2. Conditions for an efficient use would be an allocation such that $f'_2 = f'_1 + f'_2R_1$ or $f'_2 = f'_1/(1 - R_1)$; i.e., that the value of the marginal product at location (2) must be greater than the value of the marginal product at location (1) by the reciprocal of consumptive use at location (1). In general, a test of allocative efficiency between any two points i and j is that $f'_i + f'_{i+1}R_i + f'_{i+2}R_iR_{i+1} \ldots = f'_j + f'_{j+1}R_j + f'_{j+2}R_iR_{j+1} \ldots$; i.e., the value of the marginal product in the first use plus the value of the marginal product from each succeeding return flow is equal between all points of use. Consumptive use and re-use of return flow are clearly important considerations in determining allocative efficiency between two uses, which may have widely varying marginal product values as measured for diverted amounts.

EFFICENCY AND THE EXCHANGE OF RIGHTS

The preceding discussion has pertained only to tests of efficient use without regard to means of achieving changed use as the value of the marginal product declines in one use and increases in another. As previously mentioned, present western water laws recognize the interrelatedness of water supplies by protecting users' rights when a transfer occurs that changes the point or type of use.[3] However, as will be pointed out,

[3] Frank J. Trelease, *Severance of Water Rights from Wyoming Lands*, Report No. 2, Wyoming Legislative Resource Committee 1960.

present procedures have not been developed to permit a change in use of water to occur in a manner consistent with economic efficiency.

Using the example developed in the previous section, suppose the demand for water in the ith use is expanding relative to the jth use, owing to changing market conditions for the product from such use. And suppose the two parties begin negotiations for a purchase and sale transaction that would involve changing the point of diversion from j to i. The greatest amount the party at i is willing to pay is f'_i, and the least the party at j will take is f'_j. As the demand for water at i increases, presumably f'_i will increase. The greater f'_i becomes relative to f'_j the greater the incentive for a purchase transaction.

A question arises concerning the nature of the property owned by the party at j. What is the nature of the claim he has on the water resource? Almost any change in point of diversion will change the return flow pattern and pose a potential loss to someone. Therefore, a rule-of-thumb principle generally held applicable to transfers is that the amount of the transfer is restricted to the historic consumptive use. Thus, the saleable and transferable extent of ownership is different from and less than the extent of ownership for continuation in the present use. If S_j is the historical diversion at j, then the amount that i can purchase and transfer is $(1 - R_j)S_j$; i.e., the amount that has been consumptively used. In order for a sale to be feasible, $f'_i (1 - R_j)S_j$ must be greater than $f'_j S_j$ or $f'_i > f'_j/(1 - R_j)$. As previously noted, an efficient transfer would occur when $f'_i + R_i F_i > f'_j + R_j F_j$, where F_i and F_j denote the value of the marginal product for return flow users below i and j, respectively.

The permission to transfer without regard to protection of other rights would not necessarily result in an efficient allocation. The two negotiating parties consider only f'_i aid f'_j. If $R_j F_j \neq R_i F_i$, the private interests of the two parties do not result in an efficient transfer. Where $R_i F_i = R_j F_j$, the private interest of the two parties will result in an efficient transfer *under different legal codes than those which now exist*, although there would be possible third-party effects to the extent that return flows were redistributed to different users. Obviously, if the transfer occurred between basins, there would be an income transfer from one basin to the other; i.e., between return flow users.

MODIFICATION OF PRESENT PROCEDURES

To clarify the problem further and to examine some rules regarding the transfer of water from one use to another, reference is made to figure 1, which depicts certain aspects of a river system. We will consider a transfer of the right held at diversion (1) to the diversion at (3). Diversion (2) in the figure indicates many intermediate uses between (1) and (3) that are partially dependent upon the return flows from (1)

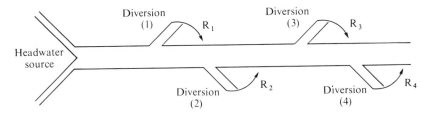

Figure 1. Schematic diagram of a simplified river system.

and exhaust the return flow; i.e., during low flows the only source of supply to the (2) users is R_1. Similarly, (4) indicates uses partially dependent on return flows from (3). If the right at (1) is transferred to (3), then the (2) users lose the R_1 return flows, and they are redistributed to the users below (3), represented in the figure by diversion (4). Present common law procedures would restrict the transfer to the historical consumptive use at (1) in order to protect the (2) rights that depend on the R_1 return flows.

A rule permitting efficient transfer is for the (3) user to be allowed to sell the return flow R_3 to downstream users (4). The (3) user could buy the return flow R_1 from the (2) users and transfer the full amount of the (1) right or leave the return flow and transfer only the consumptive use. In either case, the achievement of an efficient transfer depends on sale of R_3 to downstream users. The possibility of purchase and sale of return flows takes into account the full use of water in its present use and the full anticipated use at the new diversion. Thus, potential buyers and sellers weigh the full productive use of a given quantity of water in present and anticipated use, so that there is a possibility for the market to bring about an efficient transfer. This transfer process would be facilitated by an intermediary agency.[4] If $f'_3 < f'_1 + R_1F_2$ but $f'_3 + R_3F_4 > f_1 + R_1F_2$, then the intermediary official could inform the downstream users (4) that new water—namely, new return flow from (3)—is available for appropriation. The availability of the new water would be contingent upon the (4) users' reimbursing the purchaser (3); otherwise the transfer cannot take place. In case $f'_3 > f'_1 + R_1F_2$, the transfer can take place without the (4) users' buying (3)'s return flow; however, some method of bidding could be used to decide which (4) users get the new water.

A transfer between basins, as distinct from an intrabasin transfer, would have characteristics identical with those in the above example,

---

[4] S. E. Reynolds, State Engineer of New Mexico, indicated in private communication with the authors that his office had attempted to negotiate such a transfer.

and procedures to achieve an optimum would be the same. The assumptions in the above example were that users (2) in between (1) and (3) made full use of (1)'s return flows so that interrelatedness in supply did not extend to the (4) users, which would be the case for an interbasin transfer. That is, there would not be an interrelationship in supply between return flow users at the old and new points of diversion. Interbasin transfers would involve transportation losses, but measurement of the value of the marginal product at the point of diversion would allow a comparison between two basins.

An Example from the South Platte

As an illustration, the preceding analysis will be applied to a situation where there is an established agricultural use and a growing municipal demand. The estimates of water values in the example are applicable to agricultural use in the South Platte Valley, where the city of Denver constitutes a growing urban demand.

Municipal Denver, in the past, has not had a successful record in transferring irrigation water to add to its supply.[5] The amount it could obtain by transfer has been discouragingly small because of the return flow problem. In the 1930s the Denver Board of Water Commissioners changed its policy of trying to obtain South Platte water rights from irrigators; undoubtedly the inefficiencies in transfer procedures were a factor in that decision. The following examples suggest the magnitude of the price or cost differences engendered by the present system of transfer procedures compared with what it would be if sale of return flow were allowed.

A recent statistical analysis of land and water values in the South Platte Valley of northern Colorado indicates a capital value for agricultural use of water of approximately $36 per acre-foot.[6] Return flows from agricultural use in the South Platte have been estimated to be 50 percent,[7] and records kept by the city of Denver indicate its return flow is approximately 70 percent.[8] Referring back to figure 1, consider the city as (3) and the location of agricultural users as (1), (2), and (4), where the return flow from (1) is completely utilized by the (2) users who are junior to the (1) rights. If the city were to buy rights at

[5] Colorado State University, Economics Department, unpublished studies of Denver's attempt to transfer irrigation water, 1962.

[6] L. M. Hartman and R. L. Anderson, *Estimating Irrigation Water Values,* Agricultural Experiment Station, Colorado State University (U.S. Department of Agriculture Economic Research Service co-operating), Technical Bulletin 81, 1963, p. 19, table 5.

[7] Bureau of Reclamation, Region 7, Denver, Colo. Site selection presentation to the South Platte Steering Committee, February 1963.

[8] Denver Board of Water Commissioners, *Annual Reports,* 1900-1963.

(1), then, to protect the junior (2) users, only the historical consumptive use at (1) could be transferred to the city intakes. Assuming a 50 percent consumptive use at (1), $(1 - R_1)$, the cost of the water would be $36/0.5 = $72 per acre-foot. However, if the city could sell its newly created return flow to the (4) users at $36 per acre-foot, then the city would recover $0.7 \times \$36 = \$25.20$ per acre-foot from the first use of their return, $0.7 \times 0.5 \times \$36 = \$12.60$ from the second, and so forth. Hypothetically, the city could recover $50.40, although this would be unfeasible in a practical case. At least the logic of this procedure indicates sale of return flow sufficient to compensate losers, which is our main point.

In this example, it is assumed that adjustments are marginal to continuing agricultural production. If city purchases dried up farms, then the cost of water would reflect the resource immobilities on the farm. Alternative uses of land and improvements in a given situation determine these immobilities and consequently the value of water. A more complete discussion of this problem is presented in the last part of chapter VIII.

This example is only meant to illustrate the effect of the physical interrelatedness problem and to suggest the magnitude of the effect on actual transfers. It is not intended as a complete analysis of the factors involved in a purchase and sale transaction. It is recognized that other considerations, such as quantity of supply available for future expansion, have affected the water management policy of the city of Denver.

CONCLUSION

Several implications arise from the preceding analysis. One conclusion is that present transfer procedures do not lead to an efficient allocation of water resources except fortuitously. Also, a disregard for third-party vested rights will not necessarily ensure that transfers are efficient. On the other hand, it might be argued that since most of the anticipated transfers in water will be to municipal and industrial uses, where demands are fairly inelastic and much higher valued than in agriculture, the effects of present procedures on allocation efficiency are only slight. If demands for the higher-valued uses were completely inelastic, the effect of the present procedure would be an income transfer from higher-value users to lower-value users rather than on allocative efficiency. However, one would suppose some elasticity of demand exists for most uses within certain ranges of supply. The effect on allocation could be readily estimated if the elasticity were known.[9]

[9] For example, if the elasticity of demand for the city of Denver is −0.2, the percentage effect on allocation efficiency of present procedures is ($72.00 − $36.00)/$72.00 × 0.2 × 100 = 10 percent, using the figures from the above example. That is, the city is using 10 percent less water under present transfer procedures than it would if procedures allowed an efficient transfer.

The feasibility of a transfer procedure allowing a potential buyer to sell new return flows, which would be created further downstream, depends upon the availability of certain hydrologic data. These data would involve a knowledge of the underground geology, transmissibility of the aquifer, the water table level, etc., so that the flow from deep percolation of irrigation water could be traced in an underground basin. Most of the return flow from municipalities is returned directly into the river, so that municipal and industrial uses present no problem in terms of return flow incidence. However, in streams where pollution is a problem, measurement of return flow pollution between different uses would be necessary. Under present procedures, return flows have to be measured to some extent to determine loss to third parties, so that the procedure will not be handicapped by a complete lack of experience in collecting this type of information.

CHAPTER III

IMPLEMENTATION OF THE TRANSFER PROCESS UNDER THE APPROPRIATION DOCTRINE

Changing demands for water use are accommodated by various systems of organization: by public ownership or condemnation procedures; by the use of private market purchases and sales; or through some combination of these institutional arrangements.[1] This chapter will complement the previous one by describing and evaluating alternative procedures for the legal implementation of water transfers sought by private and public parties. The processes by which water rights are determined under the practices of the states of Colorado and New Mexico are examined in relation to the problems of establishing certainty of tenure and of facilitating transfers.[2]

It has been alleged that present laws are an obstacle to an efficient use of water because in practice protection of rights becomes a paramount concern, to the exclusion of potentially desirable transfers.[3] The analysis of the preceding chapter points up the fact that the legal rule protecting third parties is rational in an economic sense.[4] The point of view adopted in this study is that obstacles to transfers do not inhere so much in existing laws as in the uncertainties associated with the physical

[1] Stephen C. Smith, "The Rural-Urban Transfer of Water in California," *Natural Resources Journal,* March 1961.

[2] See S. V. Ciriacy-Wantrup, "Concepts Used as Economic Criteria for a System of Water Rights," *Land Economics,* November 1956, for a discussion of these two aspects of water use.

[3] See Mason Gaffney, "Diseconomies in Western Water Laws: A California Case Study" in *Conference Proceedings,* Western Agricultural Economics Research Council, Committee on Economics of Water Resource Development, January 1961. For a reply to Gaffney, see Frank J. Trelease, "Water Law and Economic Transfer of Water," *Journal of Farm Economics,* December 1961. See also Trelease, *Severance of Water Rights from Wyoming Lands,* Report No. 2, Wyoming Legislative Resource Committee, 1960, p. 29, for a discussion of common types of damage which restrict changing uses and diversion points.

[4] The present legal rule is rational as far as it goes. It does not provide for third-party gainers, who may receive newly created return flows, being brought into the transfer negotiations.

hydrologic system and the effects accompanying the transaction and that these uncertainties are affected by the procedures through which factual evidence is generated and evaluated.

Implementation of legal procedures to mediate among parties affected by water transfers involves collecting and evaluating data regarding consequences of the proposed transfers. Certain authorities are obligated to evaluate both the technical facts of the case and principles of law applicable to the specific case. Different assignments of this authority will be more or less effective in facilitating transfers depending upon how the decision-making is structured and how the available data are used. Organizations, market transactions via legal and administrative systems, and condemnation procedures all differ in these respects. Succeeding chapters present a descriptive analysis of organizational systems.

The question posed in this chapter is: Will the transfer process be better supervised by administrative agencies of state governments, or will a judicial process which depends upon state court determination be the better institutional device? Present transfer practices vary among the western states. California, Idaho, Kansas, Nebraska, New Mexico, Oregon, Utah, Texas, and Washington have administrative water control agencies empowered by law to approve or disapprove transfer and changes, after proceedings at which all interested parties are represented.[5] Colorado has a system of judicial administration with a special court procedure.[6] Arizona, Montana, Nevada, North Dakota, and South Dakota all have variations of a court procedure.[7]

BASIS FOR PROPERTY RIGHTS IN WATER

Water law in most western states has developed according to the appropriation doctrine or a modified form of riparian doctrine in conjunction with appropriation law.[8] This legal system is characterized

[5] Trelease, *Severance of Water Rights,* p. 24.

[6] Moses Lasky, "From Prior Appropriation to Economic Distribution of Water by the State via Irrigation Administration," *Rocky Mountain Law Review,* April 1929, attacked the development of appropriation law according to common law procedures as it had occurred in Colorado. He contended that the law evolving from common law procedures gave undue attention to the protection of private property rights, whereas administration of water use by a state agency under statutory law would tend to develop the use of water in the public interest.

[7] Trelease, *Severance of Water Rights,* p. 24.

[8] Wells Hutchins, "The Development and Present Status of Water Rights and Water Policy in the United States," *Journal of Farm Economics,* December 1955, and his *Selected Problems in the Law of Water Rights in the West,* U.S. Department of Agriculture Miscellaneous Publication 418, 1942. Subsequent revisions of the latter publication have appeared as separate bulletins on the water laws of each of the seventeen western states.

in large part by the doctrine that water is not legally attached to the land adjacent to it. In New Mexico water has been declared public property, but the law provides for appropriation by private parties who can demonstrate beneficial use. The state's first comprehensive statement of the law of water rights, written in 1905 during the territorial period, declared: "All natural water flowing in streams and water courses whether such be perennial or torrential, within the limits of the Territory of New Mexico, belong to the public and are subject to appropriation for beneficial use."[9] This doctrine was included in the state constitution written in 1911, where it was applied to ground water as well as surface water.

The Colorado constitution of 1876 (Article 16, Section 5) had similarly declared: "The water of every natural stream, not heretofore appropriated, within the State of Colorado, is hereby declared to be the property of the public, and the same is dedicated to the use of the people of the state, subject to appropriation as hereinafter provided."

The basis for establishing a right is essentially the same in all the western states: beneficial use of unappropriated waters. The right is specified in terms of diversion and use with a time, location, and quantity of flow dimension. The right is best characterized as a use privilege, since there is no tangible property to which ownership could be claimed. The nature of the right as a saleable entity does not become evident until a transfer of ownership is attempted. The transferred right is usually different from that of the original appropriation and depends upon both the change in use and diversion point, and effects on other users.

In the judicial process as employed in Colorado, the district courts play the primary role in determining water appropriations, water priorities, and the merits of an anticipated transfer of water rights. New Mexico, on the other hand, uses a process in which the state engineer provides the fundamental guidance in the appropriation of water rights and transfers.

In the eleven western states the only notable exceptions where transfer of irrigation water involves more complicated procedures than those reported here for Colorado and New Mexico are Arizona, Utah, and possibly Wyoming. Statutes in these states restrict water use to the lands of the original decree. Fairly recent legislation permits transfers from the original land upon petition to the state agencies.[10]

---

[9] State Engineer of New Mexico, *Twenty-Fourth Biennial Report,* November 30, 1960.

[10] R. E. Clark, ed., *Water and Water Rights* (Allen Smith, 1967), I, 353; and Trelease, *Severance of Water Rights.*

The Colorado System[11]

The system employed in Colorado to direct public waters to private beneficial use evolves through district court issuance of decrees which give to private persons the authority to develop property rights in water.

A hopeful water user in Colorado brings a private suit in the appropriate district court which requests the privilege of using waters of a given stream in a specific amount, in a specific use, and at a specific time. The petitioner is obligated to furnish evidence that there is unappropriated water available and that it will be put to beneficial use. The court clerk will have the petition advertised in the state, so that any protesting parties may be heard in the district court. The same process is followed when a party with an established water appropriation seeks to change the use of water or when a potential new user requires a change in point of diversion.

The task before the district court is to determine: (1) whether unappropriated water exists; (2) whether the petitioner will put the water to beneficial use; and (3) in case of transfers, whether the change in point of diversion will be to the detriment of established water rights. In these deliberations in Colorado, the district court is dependent upon the evidence presented by the petitioner and the protestant. The state engineer is brought into the process principally to serve as a depository for water decrees and to transfer decrees once they have been determined by the district court.

To administer the water decrees of the district courts, county commissioners appoint county water commissioners. The water commissioners allocate the water according to the decree system determined by the district court.[12] Their assignment is essentially to administer use of water within their jurisdiction as determined by the district court decrees.

Of primary concern here is the transfer of water rights rather than the original appropriation process. Interest is directed to the legal principles employed by the Colorado courts in deciding whether or not

---

[11] The authors investigated court cases involving Denver's attempts to transfer rights to its system. These cases provide a background for the discussion of this section. Transfer decrees are as follows: 411 and 582, Water District 8, District Court Files 973 and 1204, 4th Judicial District, Douglas County, February 25, 1926, and April 11, 1933; Transfer decrees 532A, 534, 538, 683, 685, 686, and 684, Water District 23, District Court Files 1212, 1974, 1936, 1973, 1975, 1976, 1977, 11th Judicial District, Park County, October 28, 1932, April 13, 1933, May 23, 1934, and April 12, 1933.

[12] Colorado is divided into seven water districts covering seven major drainage basins. These serve as administrative units within the State Engineer's Office. Each district is divided into irrigation divisions which delineate the boundaries of the water commissioner's jurisdiction.

water will be transferred from one use to another when the transfer requires a change in the point of diversion. Colorado law specifies that whenever a change in point of diversion of water is being contemplated, the party which seeks to transfer the water must bring suit in a district court in order to effect the transfer. The purpose of this litigation is to allow the court to hear all protests to the transfer so that no person with alleged property rights in the water will be injuriously affected by the transfer.

The courts, in adjudicating a case, have to develop an understanding of the physical interdependence among water users. Return flow is one very important type of interdependence. Return flow from an original appropriation gives rise to secondary appropriation which must be quantified and which the court is required to protect in the transfer decree litigation.

The courts have restricted water transfers in most cases to the volume of consumptive use when damage is proven for downstream appropriators. (Consumptive use, it will be remembered, is the difference between diversions for beneficial use and return flow.) For example, if an original appropriator has a priority for a flow of 20 cubic feet per second but historically has diverted only 10 second-feet for irrigation, the court will not allow a transfer of 20 second-feet. Rather the court will usually rule that the 10 second-feet which have not been put to beneficial use by the original appropriator has been voided by abandonment or failure to use. This means that the seller has established the right to divert a maximum of 10 second-feet, the amount of historical diversion to beneficial use. Consumptive use is not easily estimated since in irrigation it depends on crops grown, type of soil, and similar considerations. If the court decides on the basis of evidence presented that only 50 percent of the 10 second-feet beneficially used has been consumptively used, it will allow a change in point of diversion for only 5 second-feet, provided downstream damages would result from any larger diversion. Thus, it is evident that the characteristics of a transferred right are not the same as those of the historically established right but are some fraction of it.

The New Mexico System

As previously noted, the water law of New Mexico as in Colorado is based upon the doctrine of beneficial use. Beneficial use is the basis, the measure, and the limit of the right to use water. It follows, therefore, that no water right can be claimed or granted for more water than can be beneficially used.

With the exception of rights to seasonal high flows which can be captured for storage waters, the failure of any owner to use water for beneficial purposes for a period of four consecutive years constitutes forfeiture. These unused waters revert to the public except where the non-use has been caused by circumstances beyond the control of the owner.[13]

Rights to the use of water for beneficial purposes in New Mexico which existed prior to statehood were confirmed by the state constitution. After the establishment of the Office of the State Engineer all rights to the use of public waters must originate by application to that office whose functions are described as follows:

> The functions of the State Engineer's Office are defined broadly by statute. Specifically, the statutes make the State Engineer responsible for the general "supervision of the waters of the State and the measurement, appropriation, and distribution thereof." They empower him to make hydrographic surveys preparatory to adjudication of undecreed waters, to conduct studies to obtain basic hydrologic data, and to make studies of water supply and water use. Other official functions are as follows: . . . to formulate plans for the orderly development of water resources of the State; and . . . to coordinate the work of the various Federal, State, and local agencies in relation to programs of water development, conservation and use.[14]

More specifically, the State Engineer is the key public official in the supervision of the transfer of water from one place to another and from one use to another. In performing these functions the State Engineer conducts three important operations: (1) the determination of original water appropriations according to the beneficial use doctrine; (2) the determination of whether water rights can be transferred through a change in the point of diversion or change in method or place of use; and (3) the adjudication process.

The application for a right to appropriate the public waters of New Mexico must be initiated in the Office of the State Engineer. The initiation of a right by notice of intention establishes a priority date and provides the time to make the necessary surveys required by the State Engineer. Field surveys of the proposed use of the water and associated projects must be prepared by a qualified registered professional engineer, except for some minor cases where a registered surveyor may do the work.

The State Engineer arranges for publication of the proposed water

---

[13] In New Mexico the Office of the State Engineer is directly involved in the determination of continued beneficial use by the holders of water rights.

[14] State Engineer of New Nexico, *Twenty-Fourth Biennial Report,* 1960, pp. 1-2.

rights in a newspaper of general circulation within the stream system involved. The publication is continued for three consecutive weeks to inform any parties who might be adversely affected by the appropriation. The State Engineer may refuse to order the publication of notice of any application which he believes to be contrary to the public interest.

If any person or institution believes the proposed appropriation will be detrimental to a prior valid and existing right in the stream system involved, he may protest the application to the State Engineer and submit such supporting evidence as he has available. The applicant answers these protests in writing to the State Engineer and to the protesting parties. At this point the State Engineer considers the availability of unappropriated water for the proposed water right on the basis of stream flow and other available data. If he finds the results inconclusive, he sets a date and place for a formal hearing where both sides will present their cases as fully detailed by witnesses.

> In taking up an application for his decision the State Engineer shall consider whether there is any unappropriated water available; whether the applicant can satisfactorily complete the appropriation; whether the project is a feasible one; whether the building of the project be in the interest of the public. . . . If, in his opinion, there is no unappropriated water available, he shall reject such application . . .[15]

The decision of the State Engineer may be appealed to the district court within which the lands lie, the appeal to be filed within 30 days after the judgment is rendered.[16]

Substantially the same procedure as outlined above is used for changing the point of diversion and for changing the method or place of use of existing water rights. The initial application is with the State Engineer, who requires the applicant to prove no detriment to other water users.

> An appropriator, with the approval of the State Engineer, may use water for a purpose other than the purpose for which the water was appropriated, or may change the place of diversion, storage, or use, provided that no change may be allowed to the detriment of holders of valid and existing rights on the stream system.[17]

[15] State Engineer of New Mexico, *Manual of Rules and Regulations Governing the Appropriation and Use of the Surface Waters of the State of New Mexico,* 1953, p. 10.

[16] As an example of the infrequency with which decisions of the State Engineer are appealed to the district court, in the two-year period from July 1, 1958, to June 30, 1960, the legal advisors to the State Engineer of New Mexico handled only 13 surface water cases before the district court; only a small fraction of these concerned change-in-point-of-diversion litigation. The others ranged from illegal diversion and rate-of-diversion cases to contempt of court and assessments levied by the water master (*Twenty-fourth Biennial Report,* p. 31).

[17] New Mexico Statutes, Ann., 1953, Section 75-5-23.

In matters involving a change in point of diversion, place of use, or method of use, the State Engineer may hold formal or informal hearings to obtain additional evidence, may subpoena witnesses, and may require such studies as he considers necessary. The decision of the State Engineer again may be protested to the appropriate district court.

The third function of the State Engineer of interest here is the process of adjudication. The purpose of adjudication is to determine in a systematic way the current appropriation of water among the state's water users and thus the availability of unappropriated waters. Accordingly the State Engineer is directed by the courts to undertake hydrographic surveys of river basins in order to determine the nature and use of water resources.

> The statute governing the appropriation of water contains procedures for the adjudication of water rights. Such adjudications are made exclusively in the courts. Upon completion of the hydrographic survey of any stream system by the State Engineer, the Attorney General is authorized to initiate a suit on behalf of the State to determine all water rights concerned, unless such suit has been brought by private parties. Also the Attorney General is directed to intervene on behalf of the State in a suit begun by private parties, if notified by the State Engineer that in his opinion the public interest requires it. In any suit to determine water rights all claimants are to be made parties, and the court is required by statute to direct the State Engineer to furnish a complete hydrographic survey. Upon the adjudication of rights to the use of waters of a stream system a decree is issued adjudging the several water rights to the parties involved, containing all conditions necessary to define the right and its priority.[18]

The adjudication process for water rights granted since 1907 is facilitated by records of rights which have been processed through the Office of the State Engineer. Rights claimed to have existed before 1907 are more difficult. Although the adjudication can be made only by the courts, the State Engineer in his hydrographic surveys makes offers of judgment which may, and most often will, be accepted by the parties without recourse to the courts. Thus a process of clarifying existing water rights is being pursued even before the courts become involved, if indeed they ever become involved.

The State Engineer is also involved in other activities in the administrative process. He must determine: (1) what constitutes completion of a water appropriation; (2) the amount of water that can be beneficially used in various water uses; (3) the feasibility of and procedures

---

[18] Wells A. Hutchins, *The New Mexico Law of Water Rights* (U.S. Department of Agriculture, 1955), p. 37.

for diverting water out of a watershed; (4) procedures for exchanges of water; and (5) return flows from irrigation and consequent water availability.

SOME PROBLEMS IN THE TRANSFER PROCESS

One problem in the transfer process, particularly in Colorado where there is no prior adjudication of water rights, is uncertainty with regard to how rights will be quantitatively defined by the courts. This uncertainty, in turn, grows out of the physical interrelationships among water users and not out of the operations of any specific procedure. The uncertainty is caused by the different uses of water which are associated with a given set of original appropriations and which give rise to a set of return flow patterns. This set of return flows in turn gives rise to subsequent sets of secondary appropriations which, of course, vary with the availability of water as determined by return flow, storage facilities, ground water sources, precipitation, etc. This facet of uncertainty confronts any institutional system moderating the reallocation of water. One institutional system will minimize this kind of uncertainty relative to another, however, if sufficient hydrologic data are generated and used.

What is clearly lacking in Colorado are large-scale hydrographic surveys to identify the current status of water rights and water use. Such a study, conducted on a continuing basis, would provide market negotiators with information on the range in quantity of water the seller has available for sale. As it now stands, the buyer may get less than he expects when, in the transfer suit, the district court determines the amount of the original diversion right which has been abandoned and the amount above consumptive use which supplies downstream users.

Consider the impact of this uncertainty, for purposes of illustration, upon municipal agencies whose function is to project water supplies and requirements into the future. The obvious case in point in Colorado is the city of Denver. With more than 600,000 water users and with projected users in excess of one million before the end of the century, Denver has had to plan for a large expansion of its water supply. Looking back at its unpredictable and uneven success in being allowed to change points of diversion along the South Platte River, its historical water source, Denver has long since decided to seek water elsewhere and under different procedures. In the nine transfer cases brought by Denver from 1925 to 1934 to transfer 396.80 second-feet of water,[19]

[19] Transfer decrees 411 and 582, Water District 8, District Court Files 973 and 1204, 4th Judicial District, Douglas County, February 25, 1926, and April 11, 1933. Transfer decrees 532A, 534, 538, 683, 685, 686, and 684, Water District 23, District Court Files 1212, 1974, 1936, 1973, 1975, 1976, 1977, 11th Judicial District, Park County, October 28, 1932, April 13, 1933, May 23, 1934, and April 12, 1933.

only 77.39 second-feet were transferred, more than half of it in a single case. Denver has not only turned to transfers of water from the western slope of the continental divide but has also followed a policy of buying irrigation water without changing points of diversion or without using the water directly.[20]

A further examination of transfer decrees, as recorded in the State Engineer's office, reveals that only 33 municipal transfer cases, other than those for Denver, have been successfully completed. These 33 cases involve the transfer of approximately 122 second-feet from agriculture to municipal use. Of these transfers only nine have occurred since 1930.

In short, the process of water transfer in Colorado makes no provision for continuing survey and adjudication processes which attempt to provide information on the current allocative patterns of water use. In place of a continuing, state-supported hydrographic survey, Colorado employs an ad hoc, case-by-case court procedure for determining current water use patterns. The result is continuing uncertainty and confusion in the use and development of water resources.

Another facet of uncertainty which impedes efficient transfer of water in Colorado results from the way in which engineering skills are used in transfer suits when a change in point of diversion is involved. Again the State Engineer is not consulted. Rather the courts call for engineering reports from the contesting parties. The petitioner is called upon to support his set of contentions relating to return flow, and the protestants do likewise. The court, without professional engineering skills, then must make a choice or a compromise between conflicting sets of engineering data.

An interesting problem, whose existence is hinted by some evidence, is the possibility for collusion among like water users. When an agricultural user seeks to change his point of diversion, very often there are no protestants. Of course, this might be for reasons entirely different than collusion, and many times results from the lack of real effect that such a transfer has upon third-party users. But there appears to be a tendency for agricultural users to protest uniformly an agricultural-to-municipal transfer, despite the fact that some users might gain if the

[20] In analyzing the briefs and decrees of the Denver transfer cases, the reader sometimes gets the impression that Denver has acquired the permanent reputation of an unethical water-grabber and that the courts are the forum and legal skills the mechanics for disabusing city people of the notion that more water is available for municipal use. (For further discussion of the record of transfers between uses in Colorado, see the appendix to this chapter.) This may partially explain why Denver and other cities have failed to avail themselves of their legal right under Colorado law to condemn water, a process which requires the cities to compensate fully all injured parties. Such procedures should be economically efficient.

transfer were made because of the increased return flow for downstream users. In one Colorado case involving the city of Fort Collins, many downstream users who would have enjoyed an increased return flow if the city had been awarded the amount petitioned for nevertheless joined in the action as protestants to the transfer.[21]

A fourth problem is that in the transfer process in Colorado no party has the responsibility to identify and analyze the economic efficiency aspects of a proposed transfer. That is, only property rights are considered, and the concept of economic efficiency is ignored. Established property rights, obviously important, appear to be the only criteria used by the courts to determine the merits of water transfer. This is a limitation inherent in existing law and suggests that courts should be permitted to sanction a greater variety of transfers subject to full compensation to all injured parties.

CONCLUSIONS

The administrative system of New Mexico appears to offer a more efficient system for transferring water rights than the Colorado process, with its attendant uncertainty. This uncertainty, it will be recalled, has three dimensions: (1) the inherent difficulties posed by the physical interrelatedness among water users; (2) the absence of continuing hydrographic survey and adjudication processes and the consequent lack of knowledge about the actual extent of consumptive use of water in a specified use; and (3) lack of engineering data prepared by a professionally competent public agency during the course of transfer suits. In Colorado the water transfer process begins with a petition to a district court and the resultant litigation creates an adversary process from the start. In New Mexico, on the other hand, the courts are not brought into the process at all except by way of appeal in appropriation and transfer cases and directly only in the adjudication process. Instead a competent professional engineer and his professional staff are involved. They represent the public interest rather than the interests of the parties to the dispute. The availability of the courts for appeals, however, affords protection for individuals who feel strongly that their water rights have been abridged. To be sure, the parties involved in water transfers in Colorado will provide engineering data to support their positions where necessary, but the engineering studies involved necessarily are designed to prove a particular set of arguments rather than to assemble as much information as possible on a difficult area of public policy.

It is crucial for public welfare that, as water becomes increasingly

---

[21] Case No. 19347 in the Supreme Court of the state of Colorado. (See appendix to this chapter for a discussion of this case.)

scarce in relation to the demands placed upon it, the mechanism through which transfers are made be responsive to changing values in use. Continuous gathering and analysis of data, together with active negotiation among the affected parties, as in New Mexico under the Office of the State Engineer, represent a decision process more likely to lead to economically efficient decisions than the processes used in Colorado.

APPENDIX TO CHAPTER III

A Case Study of a Municipal Attempt to Transfer
Irrigation Water to Domestic Use

In chapter III some attention was paid the legal difficulties municipalities experience when they buy water rights from agricultural users and seek to transfer this water to domestic use. The nature of the adversary process thus created, the doubts and uncertainties introduced into the law of water use—in short, the whole set of rigidities incorporated into the process of water right determination—are illustrated in the case to be discussed below. This incident involved the city of Fort Collins in northern Colorado, but it is similar to a whole set of legal entanglements involving cities, specifically on the eastern slope of Colorado and generally throughout the West over the last 50 years. The problems it poses for the efficient use of water resources extend far beyond the confines of Fort Collins, Colorado.

In 1958 the city of Fort Collins agreed to purchase a water right previously used for agricultural purposes, with the intent of changing it to domestic use. In October the city filed a petition in district court requesting a change in point of diversion of this water right from the Cache La Poudre River in District 3 of Water Division No. 1. Because the legal title to these water rights was held by Lydia Hoffman Morrison and Milton Coy Hoffman and the water was being used on a farm owned by them, the case became known locally as the Coy Hoffman case. The formal legal reference is Green v. Chaffee, with Conrad C. Green listed as the first plaintiff in error and the Chaffee Ditch Company listed as the first defendant in error.

The Hoffman farm, in the bottom lands of the Cache La Poudre River, had a decree involving 15,851 cfs to irrigate 72 acres of land adjoining the river. The city purchased 8 cfs of this right and planned to change the point of diversion from the Coy ditch headgate upstream 13 miles to the city's intake.

Colorado water law states—and the courts have held—that the ownership of a water right carries with it the inherent right to change the place or character of use of the original point of diversion. However, a change in point of diversion creates problems which must be resolved before the change can legally take place. First, the determination of consumptive use at the original point of diversion and the new point of diversion must be made, involving beneficial use and return flows.

Consumptive use was earlier defined as the difference between water diverted and water which returns to the stream after use. It is that part of the water taken out of the river which is not returned to the river by return flow. Thus, in resolving this particular transfer question, it was necessary to determine the amount of water consumed historically on the Hoffman farm and in turn to determine how much water the city would use and return to the river.

Measuring the interrelatedness of water supplies—i.e., the quantity of water returning to the stream after diversion by one appropriator and subject to appropriation by others—is an important concern of the court. As noted earlier, the junior appropriators must be compensated for loss of water when transfers are made involving a change in point of diversion.

Two major problems concerned the court in the Coy Hoffman case. Was all the water—15.815 cfs—being beneficially used? And how much of the purchased water right could be transferred without injuring junior appropriators?

Addressing the first question, the protestants to this transfer, the Chaffee Ditch Company and 23 other ditch and reservoir companies, declared that the water rights on the Coy Hoffman farm had never been used for full benefit and that only part of the water necessary for irrigation of the land and historically used could be transferred without injuring other appropriators. It was found during court proceedings that Hoffman intended to continue irrigating his land with the remaining 7.815 cfs, which protestants claimed was positive and conclusive proof that the entire amount of water, 15.815 cfs, was not being beneficially used. Furthermore, protestants pointed to the fact that water would pile up 33 feet deep on the 72 acres of land if 15.815 cubic feet of water per second were diverted during the entire irrigation season.

The city of Fort Collins and seven other petitioners did not claim that the entire amount was needed to irrigate the 72 acres of land, agreeing that the Hoffmans had no right to divert 15.815 cfs for 150 days during the year or were able or disposed to do so. Petitioners did argue, however, that the water was put to a beneficial use.

Petitioners pointed out that the decree itself gave the irrigator the right to divert water at a particular time and that the needs of the land determined how long he could divert. Hoffman would apply the same amount of water on the land by diverting 15.815 cfs for 12 hours as by diverting one-half that amount for 24 hours. An early priority gave a right to put the water on quickly, and this was the right the Hoffmans were trying to protect.

Upon hearing these testimonies, the court reached the conclusion that "since not more than eight cubic feet of water per second of time could be beneficially used, all water in excess of said eight cubic feet of water per second of time has been totally and completely abandoned."

The next question to be decided by the court was whether consumptive use by the city of Fort Collins would be greater or less than water consumptively used on the Hoffman farm.

The protestants hired William E. Code to determine the farm's consumptive use. Code was well qualified in the field of ground water and had considerable experience as an officer and director of ditch companies. Upon examination of the Hoffman farm, Code found that anywhere from 1½ to 4 feet under the soil was a sandy loam, through which any water applied to the land and not consumed by plant life or evaporation would return to the river within the irrigation season. Because the Poudre River flows through this farm, the petitioners of the transfer never denied this fact.

Code then proceeded to show that water consumptively used for crops and evaporation in the Poudre River basin averaged about 1¼ acre-feet of water per acre per irrigation season. Using the Blaney-Cridell formula for determining irrigation efficiency—by which irrigation efficiency is defined to be the ratio between the amount of water consumed by the plant and by evaporation and the amount of water which must be applied to the land in order to supply this amount—he found normal irrigation efficiency in the Poudre Valley to be about 50 percent. In other words, if land has 50 percent efficiency and there were 1¼ acre-feet of consumptive use, it would be necessary to apply 2½ acre-feet of water to each acre. One-half of this would be consumed, and the balance would return to the river. Code concluded that the Hoffman farm had about 25 percent efficiency, with scattered portions of it having up to 50 percent efficiency.

On 72 acres of land, then, assuming a consumptive use of 1¼ acre-feet per acre, there would be a consumptive use of 90 acre-feet of water. If the efficiency were 25 percent, it would be necessary to apply four times that amount, or 360 acre-feet of water to supply the crop with 90 acre-feet of water. Since there would be some loss in transmission, Code determined the historic consumptive use to be about 95 acre-feet per year.

The next issue concerned the amount of water the city of Fort Collins would consumptively use; that is, how much water would return to the river from the original amount taken in at the filter plant. Any amount not returning to the stream would be considered the amount consumptively used.

The protestants again hired Code to determine the consumptive use of the city of Fort Collins. As he had already conducted studies on the return flows of sewage from the system at Thornton, Colorado, he was allowed by the court, over strenuous objections by the petitioners, to testify as to the records of the city of Thornton. Thornton was chosen because it had a tighter sewer system than that of Fort Collins, which was characterized by the protestants as being rather loose. It was Code's opinion that the actual return flow of the filtered water of the city of Fort Collins was about 35 percent.

The petitioners (for the city) used a study done in 1954-1955 by W. W. Wheeler and Associates which examined the return flow of the city of Fort Collins through the sanitary sewer system. The results of this study showed that, after correcting for outside uses and losses, the city returned 71.2 percent of the water taken into its system through the sanitary sewer. Winter months (here taken as November through March) averaged 83.4 percent, while summer months (April through October) averaged 61.4 percent.

Ironically, the city of Fort Collins furnished Code with records showing the return flow of the city's system. From these records he testified in court that city records revealed the return flow of the city to average 48.17 percent for the years 1951 through 1957.

Since estimates ranged from 35 percent to 71.2 percent, the court ruled that Fort Collins returned 50 percent of the water taken into its system from all sources to the river. Reasons for choosing the 50 percent figure were never formally given by the court.

Analysis of the Hoffman case recalls a fairly regular pattern in rural-municipal water transfers involving a change in point of diversion. Contesting parties vie before district courts on issues where contradictory technical evidence confronts the judge, who is not technically trained. A number of examples will clarify this contention.

Efforts by the contesting parties to conclusively establish the number of acres irrigated on the Coy Hoffman farm required considerable court time, involving many disagreements. Petitioners argued that 92 acres of land were irrigated, and protestants testified that 72 acres were irrigated. Testimony later revealed that the petitioners obtained their information from the county assessor's office which computed acreage by use of a 10-acre grid. Such a grid, declared the protestants, gives results close enough for tax purposes but not for this case.

Both parties spent much time and effort in preparing testimony with reference to the return flows of the city of Fort Collins. Petitioners presented as their case the Wheeler study, which concluded that the city was returning 71.2 percent of its water to the river through the sanitary sewer. At the same time city records revealing an average return flow of 48.17 percent between 1951 and 1957 were given to Code, who presented this evidence to the court. Thus, the city's own records tended to support the ultimate findings of the court, although the petitioners went to great lengths to prove otherwise.

On the same issue the protestants used as their case in point a study done by a man not familiar with municipal water systems but rather with underground water. Code was accepted by the court as an expert witness who, through a study of the sewage return of Thornton, would be knowledgeable about the sewage return of Fort Collins. This evidence obviously had a strong effect on the court, yet in no conclusive way was it demonstrated that the watering practices of the city of Thornton were similar to those of Fort Collins, that Thornton and Fort Collins had similar industrial uses, or that there existed a significant set of similarities between the two cities in other water-use variables. In fact, the witness had never investigated conditions or use of water in Fort Collins, but was permitted to take the Thornton records and apply them to Fort Collins.

Impact of the Hoffman Case on Municipal Water Policy

Following the Hoffman case, the city of Fort Collins did not attempt to buy and transfer water designated for agricultural use. Beginning in 1963, however, the city found itself short of water and established a water board to resolve the problem. Upon advice of this board and city attorneys, the city began buying water rights from farmers and ditch companies and leasing the rights back to the farmers. These were purchases of water being put to beneficial use as far as the city was able to determine—which is, of course, imperfectly.

If it is to be successful in future transfer proceedings, the city must (1) buy water where it is relatively certain that the return flow has been below the point where the city discharges its return flow, and (2) show to the court's satisfaction that its consumptive use is less than the present consumptive use, i.e., that the city will return more water to the stream after the change in point of diversion.

Fig. A-III-1 depicts the Cache La Poudre River and the points of diversion by the city and ditch companies in which the city owns stock. Defining a point of diversion as the point where the headgate of a ditch is located and water is removed from the stream, the diagram reveals that the diversion point of one ditch company (North Poudre Supply Canal) is above the city's intake, and those of four companies (Pleasant Valley and Lake Canal, Mercer, Larimer County No. 2, and Arthur) are below it. It is here assumed that all return flows will be perpendicular to the line depicting the Cache La Poudre River, an assumption which is, in most cases, factual.

The figure reveals that water purchased from appropriators in sections labeled A and B and diverted to city use would not damage downstream irrigators because return flow incidence would not be altered.

In section Z, however, return flow from Pleasant Valley and Lake Canal, New Mercer, Arthur, and Larimer County No. 2 ditches may return to the

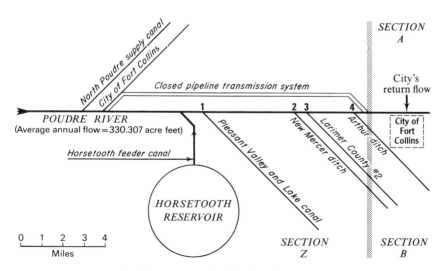

Figure A-III-1. Poudre River canal and ditch diversions.

river before the city's return flow discharge. Changing the point of diversion to the city's intake lines and transmitting this water through closed pipeline to the city will bypass these ditches and therefore eliminate some return flows upon which some water rights are based. Diverters between the city's intake and return flow discharge points could then claim damage if all or part of this return flow was being beneficially used.

For example, assume the Pleasant Valley and Lake Canal had water rights with a number one priority. The diagram shows this with a circled one at the ditch's point of diversion. Other ditches, the New Mercer, and the Larimer County No. 2, and Arthur, have priorities two, three, and four respectively. If the city buys water from the Pleasant Valley and Lake Canal Ditch Company and changes the point of diversion 12 miles upstream to its intake, no return flow will discharge into the river between that point and the city because of its closed transmission system.

The result of such a transfer would be the following. Before the transfer, ditches with priorities two, three, and four, were using water which was returning to the river from Pleasant Valley and Lake Canal with priority number one. Now, however, the water previously designated to Pleasant Valley and its number one priority would be transferred and would in turn damage water rights with priorities two, three, and four. These ditches could protest such a transfer, claiming less water available for diversion. In such cases the court will determine how much water these diverters are entitled to and will decree a particular amount to be left in the river.

The second problem facing the city, perhaps the principal issue it will face in future transfer proceedings, will be the determination of its consumptive use. In the Coy Hoffman case previously cited, the court held the city returned 50 percent of the water taken into its system to the river from all sources. This requires examination.

The return flow from the city occurs in three ways. They are: (1) sanitary sewer, (2) storm sewer, and (3) ground water. Currently, the decision of the district court appears to be conservative, in that many changes have taken place since the Hoffman case. Over 1,000 acres have been annexed to the city since 1954, and most of these have been connected to the city sewer system. Since these areas were formerly supplied with water through the city system but did not use city sewers, the percentage of return flow through the city sewer has increased.

A large amount of the city's water is returned to the river via the storm sewer. Excess water flowing into streets from lawn watering, car and street washing, and numerous other sources returns much water to the stream. There is also the return of water never entering the sanitary or storm sewers, including users not connected to the city's sewer lines and water used for lawn watering. In addition to this, the city is making constant effort to eliminate leaks in city sewer lines and so permit return flow by a more direct route and a more accurate measurement of its return.

A more realistic estimate of the city's return flow would appear to be near 75 percent of the total water taken into the system.

When initiating transfer proceedings, then, the city must be able to show the following. First, the water it has purchased is being put to a beneficial use and upon transfer of that water will continue to be put to a beneficial use. Second, the return flows of the purchased water returns to the river below the point of the city's return flow, and furthermore the city's return flows will be greater in quantity than return flows in water's previous use. As an alternative, if the river at some point is depleted because of the transfer—that is, its return flows are entering the river downstream from previous use—the city must be able to compensate those injured with water from another source.

CHAPTER IV

WATER ORGANIZATIONS:
THE MUTUAL DITCH COMPANY

One conclusion which seems to grow out of the previous discussion and the work of legal scholars who have investigated the evolution of state water law is that a high degree of rigidity has developed in the law of water rights. As we have analyzed the problem, the rigidity stems from physical externalities which pose complexities for a legal solution. Related to externalities and definition of property rights in water is lack of information on hydrologic relationships, consumptive use, and similar matters and the high cost of generating this information. The rigidity becomes effectively an economic one of providing information and the cost for private users is sufficiently high to preclude many transfers.

Yet, as one observes the actual "transferability" of water, particularly within a specified use, such as agriculture, it becomes clear that the transfer process is more responsive than an analysis of the judicial process of water transfer in Colorado suggests.

The institutional circumstance which makes water transfers more feasible than a study of water law implies appears to be the development of a set of water organizations, one result of which has been to circumvent some of the rigidities imposed by legal restraint. This element of flexibility in water transfer is the result rather than the purpose of water organizations, because it is not clear that these organizations were formed with the express purpose of providing a more flexible system for water transfer. Rather it may be that the physical externalities which explain some of the rigidities in water use were necessarily internalized in the operation of these water organizations. Thus greater transfer flexibility may be simply an effect of, rather than a purpose for, organizational experiments. On the other hand, it may have been in the minds of ditch company organizers to provide an organization permissive of greater transfer flexibility than the law provided.

However that may be, it is useful at this point to present an analysis of this type of organization by means of a case study of the North Poudre

Ditch Company of Larimer County, Colorado. Subsequent chapters will be concerned with the water conservancy district in terms of its effect on water transfers.

The relative importance of the different types of organizations involved in irrigation water deliveries is indicated by Census information on such deliveries in the 11 western states in 1964. The percentage distribution of total water deliveries is as follows: mutual unincorporated ditch companies, 9 percent; mutual incorporated companies, 32 percent; Districts, 36 percent; Bureau of Reclamation organizations, 14 percent; all others, 9 percent.[1]

The two types of organizations reported in this and the following two chapters, the mutual incorporated ditch company and the water conservancy district, involve approximately 68 percent of total irrigation water use.

THE NORTH POUDRE IRRIGATION COMPANY

Irrigation in the state of Colorado, and to some extent throughout the West, is implemented by a number of private water organizations, commonly called ditch companies. These mutual companies are usually farmer-owned associations, incorporated under state charter, whose main purpose is to supply members with water. A distinctive feature of this type of organization is its non-profit character; members are charged only what it costs to deliver and service the water.

The North Poudre Irrigation Company (NPIC) is analyzed here as a representative ditch company, typical of those found throughout the West. Its management was willing to share by interview and from records the information necessary for this analysis.

Company Organization

The NPIC was incorporated July 31, 1901, for a period of 20 years. On October 26, 1936, its stockholders passed a resolution giving the company perpetual existence. As a corporation, it can: borrow money, using the assets of the corporation as collateral; collect assessments from those stockholders who refuse to consent to needed improvements and services voted upon by the majority of stockholders; and sell those shares of stock whose assessment becomes overdue. Incorporation also permits a means of incurring obligations, entering into contracts, and appearing in court.

An incorporated ditch company operates under three basic governing sets of rules. The state corporation laws and the company's articles of

[1] See the next chapter for a discussion of a district—the Northern Colorado Conservancy District—which is an example of a general type.

incorporation act as its basic constitution and function as its external authority. Internally a company's bylaws and the minutes of each meeting become the governing rules for water delivery. Each must be examined in terms of its basic function.

Article 14 of the 1963 Colorado Revised Statutes states that an incorporated ditch company must specify the source, point, and place from which water is taken, the location of any reservoir in existence or to be constructed, and the intended use of all such water. A company has the legal power to make an assessment on its capital stock, specify to whom the water will be furnished, and bind itself by mortgaging its irrigation works. A mutual ditch company under these laws is exempt from income tax, both state and federal, providing that 85 percent or more of its gross income consists of money collected for the sole purpose of meeting expenses and operating losses.

The objectives and purposes of the NPIC as stated in its articles of incorporation are:

1. To acquire the canals, reservoirs, and lands situated in Larimer County in the State of Colorado, together with all rights, rights of way, reservoir sites, privileges, franchises, and appropriations of water from the North Fork of the Cache La Poudre River and its tributaries.

2. To construct six reservoirs for storage of water for irrigation, and to acquire, own, and operate the property and necessary ditches for the carriage and distribution to said reservoirs.

3. To acquire further appropriations of water for irrigation by canals and reservoirs from the Cache La Poudre River.

4. To acquire lands for rights of way for its canals, inlet, supply, and lateral ditches by grant, purchase, condemnation, or otherwise, and buy other waters to apply to the lands owned by the stockholders.

5. To promote the foregoing purposes by exercising all powers necessary for the development and successful operation of said enterprise.

Bylaws govern the relations between stockholders and officers. These laws are enacted by the stockholders and provide a flexible instrument for the operation of the company. Many of the internal rules for delivering water are found in these laws, as well as amount of capital stock, duties of officers and committees, election, powers, and duties of the board of directors, officers, and employees, rates of compensation, and other rules pertaining to the operation of the company.

NPIC has an authorized capitalization of $500,000 which, in essence, represents the value of the physical property as well as the water rights acquired by the company. This capital is represented by shares of stock owned by 324 individual shareholders. Since 1901, 10,000 shares of stock have been sold, ranging from a quarter share on small tracts to 466 shares on large farms. These shares of stock represent a right to receive water as well as to become a part owner of the company. In terms of water supply, each share of stock represents 1/10,000 of the company's total water supply measured in acre-feet.

At the company's inception each share of stock had a par value of $50.00. The present par value is $300.00. Bearing little relation to par value is a share's market value, the price determined by market forces for which a share of stock can be sold. The following table shows the number of shares transferred for the years 1960 through May of 1966. The prices at which shares sell are not given, since the company keeps no records of these sales, although most of the transactions take place through the company. Management knows that in some instances shares are given away, as in cases of long-time neighbors, and in others as much as $800.00 per share is received. Generally, however, the price per share averaged $200.00 in 1960, $375.00 in 1963, and between $500.00 and $600.00 in 1965.

TABLE 1. NPIC SHARE TRANSFERS, 1960-1966

Year	Number of shares transferred	Number of transactions	Transactions involving two shares or less
1960	344	21	3
1961	415	23	4
1962	967	29	3
1963	1,350	68	17
1964	1,104	64	21
1965	990	71	26
1966 (May)	629	27	2
Total	5,789	303	76

Source: Files of the North Poudre Irrigation Company, Wellington, Colo.

Water Supply and Physical Facilities

The principal sources of water supply for the NPIC are the main Cache La Poudre River and its North Fork. From these sources water becomes available to the stockholders of the NPIC by direct flow, storage, and the mountain system. In addition the company has water rights in Horsetooth Reservoir, a part of the Colorado-Big Thompson project. Direct flow refers to water decreed in the 1860s and 1870s from the two rivers. The following table shows the priority of the decrees and the second-feet of water available which can be used beneficially upon the land, but not for storage.

TABLE 2. NPIC DIRECT-FLOW DECREES

Priority	Date	Amount in second-feet	Priority	Date	Amount in second-feet
3	6/1/1861	0.72	63	9/1/1873	11.00
17	4/15/1866	4.75	69	5/15/1874	3.32
19	7/1/1866	2.165	77	5/1/1875	6.72
29	6/1/1868	2.165	79	6/1/1876	6.72
59	7/1/1873	7.20	80	6/1/1876	6.72
61	7/15/1873	9.38	82	6/1/1877	2.85
63	8/15/1873	3.32			

Source: The North Poudre Irrigation Company, Wellington, Colorado.

All 13 of these decrees are good water rights until approximately the middle of June. Then, as the river level declines, priorities 59 through 82 are seldom deliverable. Horsetooth Reservoir water is diverted from Lake Granby on the western slope of Colorado through the Colorado-Big Thompson project administered by the Northern Colorado Water Conservancy District. This water has been used since 1953.

The NPIC owns 24 storage reservoirs with a total decree capacity of 74,855 acre-feet and approximately 200 miles of ditches that vary in size from laterals a few feet wide to canals with a bottom width of 24 feet. Approximately 10 percent of its canals are lined to prevent seepage, and 5 miles of ditches use concrete pipe. The company gets none of its water from pumping underground water. The mountain system refers to water coming from a ditch and a lake the company owns in the mountains between Cameron Pass and Chambers Lake. During the period 1961-64, an average of 87,146 acre-feet of water was available to NPIC from all sources. Storage yielded 51.4 percent; direct flow, 10.7 percent; Horsetooth Reservoir, 37.7 percent; and the mountain system, 0.2 percent.

Company Operations

All activities are complementary to the delivery of water to member stockholders. Operation and maintenance, then, become the primary function of the NPIC and account for the greater part of its budget.

Water assessments are the company's exclusive source of income. They provide funds for: wages of employees, officers, and directors; cost of maintaining ditches and reservoirs; purchase of equipment, and paying off loans and interest. If the stockholders accept the board of directors' recommendations, water is allocated equally among the shares of stock and the expenses are correspondingly prorated. Table 3 shows the water assessment for 1965 and assessments per share for the years since 1909.

TABLE 3. NPIC ASSESSMENTS, 1965, BY OBJECTIVE, AND YEARLY ASSESSMENTS, 1909-1965

1965 ASSESSMENT

	Per share	Total
Water assessments[a]	$ 6.25	$ 62,500.00
Maintenance and operation	7.00	70,000.00
New equipment	.75	7,500.00
Weed control	1.00	10,000.00
Park Creek survey	1.00	10,000.00
Total	$16.00	$160,000.00

YEARLY ASSESSMENTS

Year	Assessment	Year	Assessment	Year	Assessment
		1926	$ 5.00	1946	$ 7.25
		1927	8.00	1947	9.00
		1928	8.50	1948	13.00
1909	$ 5.00	1929	8.25	1949	12.00
1910	5.00	1930	8.25	1950	12.00
1911	4.00	1931	7.50	1951	12.00
1912	5.00	1932	7.00	1952	12.00
1913	6.00	1933	4.50	1953	14.40
1914	7.00	1934	5.00	1954	18.60
1915	7.00	1935	4.25	1955	18.00
1916	7.00	1936	6.00	1956	16.00
1917	7.00	1937	5.75	1957	9.00
1918	7.00	1938	6.75	1958	15.00
1919	8.00	1939	7.75	1959	14.50
1920	11.00	1940	7.25	1960	14.50
1921	8.00	1941	4.00	1961	14.50
1922	6.50	1942	6.25	1962	14.50
1923	6.50	1943	8.00	1963	14.50
1924	9.50	1944	7.25	1964	15.00
1925	12.00	1945	7.25	1965	16.00

Source: North Poudre Irrigation Company, Annual Report, year ending December 31, 1965, p. 20.
[a] Collection from stockholders to pay for Colorado Big Thompson water delivered by NCWCD.

Dividends in the form of acre-feet of water per share are generally declared by the board of directors three or four times per growing season. The average total dividend for the period 1930 through 1952 (prior to the availability of Horsetooth water) was 2.5 acre-feet of water per share. During the period of 1953-1964 the average total dividend was 5.2 acre-feet of water per share.

The dates in table 4 refer to stockholder meetings when the dividends are declared. It shows, for example, that dividends of 2, 1, 1, and 1 acre-feet of water were declared on April 26, June 8, July 7, and August 4, 1965, respectively. In order that water be used when it is in the river, the following provisions are usually applied:

30 percent must be used before July 1;
50 percent must be used before August 1;
70 percent must be used before September 1.

TABLE 4. NPIC DIVIDENDS, 1965

Date	Acre-feet of water per share
August 4, 1965	1.0
April 26, 1965	2.0
June 8, 1965	1.0
July 7, 1965	1.0
	5.0

Source: North Poudre Irrigation Company, *Annual Report,* year ending December 31, 1965, p. 3.

In other words, 3 acre-feet of water were declared available in 1965 for every share of stock before July 1, at least 30 percent of which must have been used by that time. Through August 4, 1965, 5 acre-feet of water per share were declared available, at least 70 percent of which had to be used before September 1.

Ownership

Almost 95 percent of the stockholders of the NPIC are engaged in farming. These 324 individual shareholders own either individually or in partnership a total of 308 holdings which average approximately 110 acres in size. Only eight exceed 160 acres per individual. (Holdings reported in table 5 may be in multiple ownership.)

Most of the farms in the NPIC have facilities for livestock operations but only a few are sizeable operations. Livestock average less than 60 head per farm, and they are generally fed on non-irrigated pasture lands

TABLE 5. HOLDINGS IRRIGATED UNDER NORTH POUDRE IRRIGATION SYSTEM, 1964

Holding size (acres)	Number of holdings	Total area (acres)
0-20	85	600
21-40	14	485
41-80	51	3,297
81-120	39	4,040
121-160	71	10,530
161-240	24	4,895
241-320	13	3,820
321-480	5	2,080
481-640	1	630
641 & over	5	3,420
Total	308	33,797

Source: Files of the North Poudre Irrigation Company, Wellington, Colo.

associated with the farm. Besides the city of Fort Collins and the East Larimer Water District, which together own less than 7 percent of the total number of shares, all of the NPIC stockholders own irrigable land. All water users are members and shareholders of the company.

WATER TRANSFERS WITHIN DITCH COMPANIES

Because of the varying circumstances and corresponding rules for transferring water from user to user and company to company, other ditch companies will be included in this section for purpose of comparison. The irrigation companies in the South Platte River basin are rather liberal in their water transfers; farmers can pass them freely from one tract of land to another without serious interference by the company. This result has stemmed from rental arrangements under which water can be transferred to a higher use through and by the market process.

Rental arrangements are the institutional channels by which water is transferred from user to user during a single irrigating season. Renting water in the South Platte basin is possible for a number of reasons. First, almost all large irrigation companies own their own storage reservoirs, which provide a means of storing water, by decrees and runoff, which becomes a valuable addition for late summer needs. Second, the water rights are owned by the ditch company and are not connected to any tract of land. Such an arrangement permits transfers within the service area which probably would not occur had the right been owned or appurtenant to land. A third reason why water can be rented stems from the availability of water from the Colorado-Big Thompson diversion project, which can be transferred anywhere within the Northern Colorado Water Conservancy District, a feature to be discussed in some detail in chapter V.

Large irrigation companies such as the NPIC maintain a rental service in their offices, where users with an excess supply post the asking price and number of shares they have for rent. Buyers contact the company secretary for this water. Other companies simply allow the individual farmers to arrange their water transfers as well as asking price. Both reservoir and direct flow water are rented, depending on the facilities of the company. Table 6 illustrates the various procedures.

A study of water rentals by Raymond L. Anderson showed that in 1959 five irrigation companies were involved in 645 transfers involving 16,353 acre-feet of water.[2] Most of these rentals take place in the peak irrigation season during the months of July, August, and September. Table 7 shows that most water rentals were small in quantity, 74.5 percent

[2] Raymond L. Anderson, "The Irrigation Water Rental Market: A Case Study," *Agricultural Economics Research,* June 1961.

TABLE 6. WATER-RENTAL PROCEDURES IN THE SOUTH PLATTE BASIN, COLORADO

Company and location	Method of renting	Method of pricing	Kind of water rented
North Poudre Irrigation Co., Ft. Collins	Water for rent is listed on a board in office. Buyers contact secretary for water.	Asking price quoted along with number of shares each individual has for rent	Shares of stock including direct-decree and reservoir water are rented
Larimer and Weld Ditch, Eaton	Available water is listed in company office. Secretary allocates to those wanting additional water.	Board of Directors sets price for season	Reservoir water rented by day's run
New Cache La Poudre Irrigating Co., Greeley	Available water is listed in company office. Buyers contact secretary for water.	Secretary and Board of Directors set price for season	Reservoir water rented by day's run. Few shares of direct flow rented each season
Water Supply and Storage Company, Ft. Collins	Shares of seasonal water rented from office. Small daily transfers are traded between farmers.	Farmers set the price of both seasonal and daily rental	Both direct-decree water and reservoir water are rented by the day and by the share
Bijou Irrigation District and Riverside Irrigation Co., Ft. Morgan	Farmers arrange for transfers. Transfer orders are recorded in office.	Farmers negotiate price when arranging transfer.	Mostly reservoir water by the share, but some direct decree water when farmer has well.
Farmers Reservoir and Irrigation Co., Denver	Most water rented between farmers. Must submit water transfer order to company files.	Farmers set price.	Rent stock or acre-feet. Most rentals are reservoir water.

Source: Raymond L. Anderson, "The Irrigation Water Rental Market: A Case Study," Agricultural Economics Research, June 1961.

TABLE 7. NUMBER AND AMOUNT OF WATER-RENTAL TRANSFERS IN FIVE IRRIGATION COMPANIES, SOUTH PLATTE BASIN, 1959

Size of transfer	Transfers	Cumulative percentage	Amount of water	Cumulative percentage
Acre-feet	Number	Percent	Acre-feet	Percent
0 to 9.9	175	27.1	977	6.0
10 to 19.9	180	55.0	2,430	20.9
20 to 29.9	126	74.5	3,084	39.6
30 to 39.9	56	83.2	1,872	51.2
40 to 49.9	33	88.3	1,426	59.9
50 to 59.9	29	92.8	1,604	69.7
60 to 69.9	9	94.2	564	73.1
70 to 79.9	10	95.8	759	77.7
80 to 89.9	5	96.6	420	80.3
90 to 99.9	1	96.8	96	80.9
100 to 149.9	14	99.0	1,774	91.6
150 to 199.9	4	99.6	681	95.9
200 plus	3	100.0	666	100.0
Total	645		16,353	

Source: Raymond L. Anderson, "The Irrigation Water Rental Market: A Case Study," *Agricultural Economics Research*, June 1961.

involving fewer than 30 acre-feet of water. These transactions represented transfers between farmers within their respective companies.

The price of water rented during the early irrigation season is similar to what a member would pay for his allotment. During dry years and late in the irrigation season, however, the price of rental water increases considerably and is held down only by community pressure and institutional restraints. Many times the rental price is set below what a farmer would be willing to pay, which at times is reported to be as high as $30 per acre-foot, and rental rates have increased in recent years.

COMPANY-TO-COMPANY RENTAL ARRANGEMENTS

The establishment and development of ditch companies in the Cache La Poudre River basin included unique features. Most of these companies were founded by local farmers, who upon settlement claimed as much water through direct flow appropriation and reservoir rights as possible. The result of such action was ownership of reservoirs far distant from company lands, often downstream from its ditches and canals. Because of these historical and developmental procedures water must be traded to be utilized.

The NPIC is a good example. It owns a reservoir near Timnath, Colorado, which it could not possibly use in its system. These 12,000 acre-feet of water, lying far below the company's ditches and canals, must be traded for water owned by another company which the NPIC can use. These trades are handled through the company, administered by the water commissioner, and occur seasonally rather than permanently. In this instance, a number of ditch companies near Timnath can use this reservoir water. They in turn own direct flow rights in the Cache La Poudre River or reservoir water above the NPIC's system. These companies contact each other and make arrangements for trading reservoir water for direct flow rights, or reservoir water for reservoir water. The water commissioner administers these trades by notifying each company as to the amount of water it is entitled to in direct flow rights and the amount of water measured in their reservoirs to be traded.

Seasonal rather than permanent transfers occur for two reasons. First, the amount of water in a reservoir varies from year to year, thus placing a company in a different bargaining position. Most stockholders feel they are better off with the reservoir they own. The second reason can be attributed to the stockholders' unwillingness to ratify permanent changes. Stockholders are suspicious of any type of reorganization, including reservoir changes, and incidents such as the discovery of oil on a reservoir site formerly owned by the company have solidified stockholders' reluctance to ratify permanent transfer. Seasonal trades, then, are confirmed by letter year after year, with little chance of becoming permanent.

CONCLUSIONS

One obvious and compelling conclusion of this study of ditch companies is that they facilitate economically efficient use of water within their area. One could argue there is no *obvious* institutional restraint on the operation of competitive market forces for allocating water resources within the company itself. The process of purchase and sale of stock and seasonal renting should meet the test of a near-perfect market. Information on water deliveries per share of stock, on stock for sale, and on rental water available is easily disseminated through the company system. There is no restraint on purchase and sale of the resource except the willingness of the parties involved. Also, the practice of rentals, where they are physically feasible, between users in different companies permits limited market forces to effect some efficiency through the larger confines of a basin.

However, the question of basin-wide efficiency between different uses and between different company areas is little affected by the company form of organization. The mobility of the resource in this context is subject to the judicial transfer process as discussed in chapter III. Whether this process works more effectively with a mutual company holding the rights than with an individual is a question outside the purview of our analysis.

CHAPTER V

WATER ORGANIZATIONS: THE NORTHERN COLORADO WATER CONSERVANCY DISTRICT

Another organizational form which warrants detailed study is the water conservancy district, which developed many years after the mutual ditch company. The concept of the water conservancy district in Colorado originated during the years of severe drought in the 1930s which exacerbated one of the state's basic water problems. This problem stems from the fact that there is more precipitation west of the continental divide but more irrigable land and more population east of the divide. It had long been perceived that transfer of water from the western slope would offer a partial solution to eastern slope problems if a way could be found to finance the costly engineering required to achieve transfer, which was beyond the legal and fiscal capacities of such private organizations as the ditch company. The obvious source of funding was the federal government which, under the Reclamation Act of 1902, could build projects whose costs would be repaid in part by users of the water developed.

The organizational response to the problem was the creation of the water conservancy district as a public agency through which individual and corporate water users could contract to repay to the federal government a share of the costs of the project. The conservancy district would also administer the allocation of project water.

This chapter will examine the Northern Colorado Water Conservancy District, which was the prototype organization.[1] Although its original objectives and subsequent operations have been primarily to develop water and repay part of the costs of the reclamation project on which it is based, certain features of the District allow a water market to function.

THE COLORADO-BIG THOMPSON PROJECT

From as early as 1881, engineering studies had been conducted to

---

[1] For a historical account, see J. M. Dille, *A Brief History of Northern Colorado and Colorado-Big Thompson Project* (The District, 1958).

determine the feasibility of diverting water from the Colorado River watershed on the western slope to the South Platte River watershed on the eastern slope. In 1933, serious efforts were exerted to interest the U.S. Bureau of Reclamation in such a project, and in December 1934 the Northern Colorado Water Users Association was incorporated to act as the promotion agency.

As might be expected, the new association faced serious opposition by water users on the western slope, who formed the Colorado River Protective Association under the leadership of Congressman Edward T. Taylor. Taylor was in a strategic position as chairman of the Appropriations Committee of the House of Representatives. The basic position of the association was that, before water could be diverted from the Colorado, storage facilities must be built on the western slope to develop and retain an amount of water equal to that which it was proposed to divert.

Late in 1936, Colorado's State Planning Commission undertook a complete economic survey of northern Colorado to estimate the value of the proposed diversion from local, state, and national standpoints. The survey covered northern Colorado in terms of the water supplies then existing, the economic losses attributable to lack of water, and contemplated developments in the area based on availability of supplemental water.

In 1937, the two associations reached an agreement on the construction of an adequate reservoir on the western slope and stipulations regarding its operation. In July of that year, Senator Alva B. Adams, chairman of the Senate Committee on Irrigation and Reclamation, introduced a bill to authorize the Colorado-Big Thompson project. The bill passed later in the summer authorized construction of dams and storage reservoirs on the Colorado River watershed and a 13-mile tunnel under the continental divide to transfer supplemental water to tributaries of the South Platte.

THE CONSERVANCY DISTRICT ACT OF 1937

While the Colorado-Big Thompson project was being considered in Congress, a bill to authorize conservancy districts was placed before the Colorado General Assembly and became law on May 13. The Conservancy District Act then successfully passed court examination to determine its constitutionality.[2]

The Act provides for the organization of districts by means of a petition to a district court, to be signed by at least 1,500 owners of irrigated land and 1,000 owners of non-irrigated land. Boards of directors are

2 *Ibid.*, pp. 20-23.

appointed by the courts hearing petitions.[3] These boards have the power to appoint officers, acquire and hold property, appropriate water, enter into contracts, levy assessments and taxes, allot water, and administer any other business of the districts. The boards are specifically empowered to levy ad valorem taxes on all real and personal property lying within District boundaries which receives indirect benefits. Further provisions of the Act are for individual water allotments and allotments to municipalities. Special assessments are levied for these uses of water. The boards of directors also have the power, under authorization of property owners, to negotiate or to contract with the United States for construction of works.

ORGANIZATION OF THE NORTHERN COLORADO WATER CONSERVANCY DISTRICT

Following the passage of the Conservancy District Act, the Northern Colorado Water Conservancy District (NCWCD) was formed. The boundaries of the District were determined and the areas which were to help pay project costs were named. The District in its final form had an area of 2,315 square miles, somewhat larger than the state of Delaware. Seven counties—Boulder, Larimer, Weld, Morgan, Washington, Logan and Sedgwick—were originally included in the District. Washington County is no longer a member.

Upon approval of the proposed District area, a petition was drawn up for presentation to the District Court of Weld County for the formal organization of the District, and the requisite number of signatures was obtained. The hearing, set for the Weld County Court for September 1937, produced no opposing petitions, and the NCWCD was established and members of the board of directors appointed.

Following organization and upon successful completion of a test for constitutionality, the District began negotiation of a contract for partial repayment of federal expenditures on the Colorado-Big Thompson project. Such repayment is one of the District's main functions. Aspects of the contract that are of interest here may be briefly summarized as follows:

1. A description of the major construction, designed to deliver an average of 310,000 acre-feet of water into the St. Vrain, Little Thompson, Big Thompson, and Cache Poudre rivers;

2. Provisions concerning allocation of costs and terms of payment by which the District would pay one-half of the construction costs—but not to exceed $25,000,000—in 40 years, without interest, under a

[3] *Northern Colorado Water Conservancy District and Colorado-Big Thompson Project: Progress Report* (The District, January 1954).

schedule which initially required $450,000 annually for the first 20 years; $500,000 annually for the third 10-year period; and one-tenth of the balance annually for the fourth 10-year period;

3. Stipulations as to the maximum tax levies and assessments the District could make and for the application of the funds collected;

4. The disposition of expected return flows from project supplies.[4]

When it became evident that there was going to be a wide discrepancy between estimated and actual costs, the Bureau of Reclamation attempted to obtain a revision of the contract's repayment terms. The District refused to renegotiate on the grounds that the contract had been formulated on the basis of Bureau recommendations and that large quantities of water had been allotted under contract at a definite rate of assessment. Further, the intent of the contract had been approved by the taxpayers and voters of the District and any attempt to increase the rates of assessment would meet with strong opposition and probable defeat. The federal government has thus been faced with recovering the additional costs of the project through revenue from power generating plants and, despite the agreement of the District to repay an additional $3 million, the major part of the cost remains the responsibility of the United States. The cost responsibility assumed by NCWCD was approximately 15 percent of the total cost of the project. The final cost of the project was $161.6 million, compared to the estimate in 1937 of $44 million.

ALLOCATION OF COSTS AND COLLECTION OF REVENUES

The District board members are empowered by statute to allocate water supplies among users entering into contract with the District. As agreed upon in the contract, water allocations are made at a charge of $1.50 per acre-foot. An ad valorem tax of one-half mill per annum was set on all real and personal property within the District for the period preceding District water delivery, to be raised to one mill per annum after deliveries had begun. The justification for the mill-levy stems from the fact that water being delivered to the various communities provides certain benefits to those communities regardless of use— domestic, irrigation, or industrial.

There are five contract classes from which District revenue is obtained

---

[4] This was a major problem in establishing the contract. Some Bureau officials thought that the District should collect revenue from persons receiving the benefits of return flows, primarily to provide an additional source of revenue to strengthen the District's ability to repay. However, the District officials felt this plan would be impracticable to administer and enforce.

Article 19 of the contract stipulates that rights for return flows are left to the District for recapture and re-use. There is, however, a discrepancy in the views taken toward the sale of return flows, as noted in a subsequent section of this chapter.

at fixed rates. These are: (1) Class B, Municipal Contracts; (2) Class C, Irrigation District Contracts; (3) Class D, Private Irrigation Contracts; (4) Section 25 Contracts with corporations and ditch companies; and (5) Temporary Use Permits which allow a city to obtain the use of water on a yearly basis until such time as the city uses water on this basis to warrant a permanent transfer of water.

The revenue that can be obtained from these contract classes is, in general, inflexible. However, the revenue obtainable from the ad valorem tax will increase or decrease with general economic trends and will produce more revenue for NCWCD as the assessed value of property within the District increases.

Two revenue questions face the Board of Directors of the NCWCD. The first is whether the revenue obtained from the ad valorem tax and the fixed-rate water agreements together will meet the remaining obligations of repayment under the contract. The second question is, in case the present revenue sources are insufficient, how additional revenue can be obtained from District operation. Appendix tables A-V-2, A-V-3, and A-V-4 summarize present and projected costs and revenues. Table A-V-5 shows an expected shortage of revenue by 1982. This possibility has led the Board of Directors to suggest that any future contracts with corporate enterprise or with municipalities contain provisions granting contract reviews and possible rate changes at the Board's discretion.

DISPOSITION OF RETURN FLOWS

An item of concern in the repayment contract is the disposition of return flows from project water. The contract is somewhat confusing, as it states two different views on the subject of return flows.

The position of the United States, as stated in Article 19 of the contract, is as follows: "There is also claimed and reserved by the United States for the use of the District for domestic, irrigation and industrial uses, all of the increment, seepage and return flow water which may result from the construction of the project and the importation thereby . . . from the Colorado River watershed . . . ; and the right is reserved on behalf of the District to capture, recapture, use and re-use the said added supply . . ." Further, "Any overplus of such captured, recaptured and return flow water shall be rented, sold or disposed of for domestic, irrigation and industrial uses within the District, at such times, under such conditions and upon such terms as the Board of Directors of the District may, from time to time, determine."

The same article states that: "Said captured, recaptured and return flow water shall be, by the Board of Directors, allocated only to the irrigable lands within the District already being partially supplied with

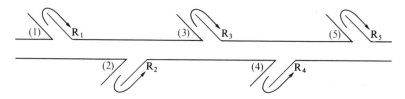

Figure 2. Simplified river system with diversions and return flows.

water for irrigation, using as a basis for such allocation the decreed
priorities existing at the date of this contract, and without other or
additional consideration of payments by the owners of such lands . . ."

In order to understand the District's position on this problem, consider the simplified river system in figure 2, where numbers designate
diversions and R return flows. Assume that (1), (2) and (4) are
District water users, while users (3) and (5) are allotted water according to original decrees. How are the return flows used when they enter
the system? Can the District bypass (3) and (5) in moving return
flows from District water to users downstream?

The position taken by the United States is that the return flows remain
District property and can thus be allotted by the District. The District,
under this position, could sell return flows to anyone showing beneficial
use for the flows. According to the United States, return flow water
from the project could bypass (3) and (5) and be sold to another
downstream District water user.

The District has maintained that return flows, once they re-enter the
river system, become a part of the stream flow. The return flows may
then be appropriated by existing river decree according to the highest
priority. User (3) then has the right to use the return flows from (1)
and (2) in the amount allotted under his decree. The same holds true
for (5) in the use of return flows from (4). The District itself has, then,
denied its right to bypass users (3) and (5) in the sale and transfer of
return flows from project water to downstream District water users.
In effect the return flow from District water provides a windfall gain to
decree rights by augmenting the river flow. The main beneficiaries are
junior appropriators, and the water commissioner, managing the river
as a system, can make maximum use of return flow by anticipating
buildup of returns downstream as the season progresses.

It can be argued that the District does have a legal right to sell or
rent return flows from project water diversions, since this right was given
to the District by the United States in the repayment contract. The
District has not followed this policy for two main reasons. First, it would
be contrary to the water law of the state, which requires that return

flows become a part of the stream flow. Second, it is difficult to measure return flows and to determine the point of re-entry into the stream. Not only must quantity of return flows be determined, but quality must be considered as well.

ALLOCATION OF DISTRICT WATER

The relationship between water users and the District is a contractual one. The procedure followed in the NCWCD allotment process was as follows: (1) an allotment of water required a contractual agreement between the petitioner (water user) and NCWCD; (2) the petitioner made application to the District for a specified quantity of water to be used for a specified purpose on a specified tract of land; and (3) the petitioner had to satisfy the District officials that there was an actual need for the water and that the water was going to be put to a beneficial use. The third condition did not apply to municipalities.

There were no considerations of priority in allotting District water in the early years of operation. Once the District had determined that the water would be put to beneficial use and that the amount of water applied for was not excessive, the petition was granted. However, in 1953, when it became evident that the District was nearing its allotment quota of 310,000 acre-feet, the dating of applications began. When the Board reviewed the applications, it gave those bearing no dates priority over those which were dated. From then on, those applications bearing the earliest dates were given consideration before those with later dates.

Table 8 presents the original water allotments made by the District in 1955. The total allotments are separated into individual allotments according to water district[5] and the number of contracts held in each contract class. The table depicts the number of acre-foot units, by river basin and contract class, and the final column gives the percent of District allotments held by each of the six river basin areas.

In 1955 there were 2,631 Class D Contracts which involved a total of 197,340 acre-feet of water used for private irrigation. There were nine Class B Contracts, involving 44,950 acre-feet of water for domestic water use in municipalities. The one Class C Contract was for 6,000 acre-feet of water to be used for irrigation; this contract is in the possession of Riverside Irrigation District in Morgan County. Section 25 Contracts serve various uses. In 1955, three of the seven contracts in this class were held by manufacturing concerns and involved 3,000 acre-feet of District water. The remaining contracts involved 58,710 acre-feet of water which were used for irrigation. Of the total amount of water available for allotment in 1955, NCWCD allotted 84.53 percent

---

[5] For definition of water district, see chapter III, fn. 12.

TABLE 8. NORTHERN COLORADO WATER CONSERVANCY DISTRICT WATER ALLOTMENT SUMMARY, BY RIVER BASIN AND CONTRACT CLASS, 1955

River basin	Class D number	Class D acre-feet	Class B number	Class B acre-feet	Class C number	Class C acre-feet	Section 25 number	Section 25 acre-feet	Total acre-feet	Percent of NCWCD water
Cache la Poudre	980	85,343	2	21,000	—	—	5	43,380	149,723	48.3
Big Thompson	988	67,264	3	5,900	—	—	2	1,510	74,694	24.1
St. Vrain	466	32,892	3	5,350	—	—	1	500	38,742	12.5
Boulder Creek	142	8,025	1	12,700	—	—	—	—	20,725	6.7
Middle S. Platte	8	910	—	—	—	—	1	10,320	11,230	3.6
Lower S. Platte	47	2,906	—	—	1	6,000	1	6,000	14,906	4.8
Total	2,631	197,340	9	44,950	1	6,000	10	61,710	310,000	100.0
Percent of total allotment		63.7		14.5		1.9		19.9		100.0

Source: Official records of the District, Loveland, Colo.
Note: For definition of classes, see text.

(262,050 acre-feet) to irrigation uses, 0.967 percent (3,000 acre-feet) to manufacturing uses, and 14.48 percent (44,905 acre-feet) to domestic uses.

In 1964, there were 2,889 Class D Contracts, an increase of 258 contracts over the number held in 1955; but the amount of water allotted under this contract class decreased to 188,451 acre-feet, a decrease of 8,889 acre-feet. Class B Contracts increased to 12 in number and to 45,976 acre-feet for domestic use. There was no change in the Class C Contract. The 33 Section 25 Contracts held in 1964 included 71,563 acre-feet. Eight of the contracts called for 6,155 acre-feet for domestic use, and three of them used 3,590 acre-feet for manufacturing. Twenty-two of the contracts (excluding state-owned land) were allotted 57,818 acre-feet of water for irrigation. The remaining nine contracts were those for state-owned land, and these were allotted 900 acre-feet of water.

In 1960, the District initiated a new type of contract, the Temporary Use Permit, which allows municipalities to request the yearly use of small quantities of water. After a specified quantity of water is obtained, the municipality may petition for a permanent reallocation or transfer of the water. There were four such contracts in 1964, amounting to 1,110 acre-feet of water for domestic purposes.

In 1964, the NCWCD allotted 253,169 acre-feet of water to be used for irrigation. This was 81.67 percent of the total available for allotment but was 3.42 percent less than the amount of water allotted for the same purpose in 1955. The Board allotted 53,241 acre-feet of water, or 17.17 percent of the supply available, to 24 contracts for water used for domestic purposes. This was an 18.56 percent increase over 1955. Manufacturing concerns held three contracts that totaled 3,950 acre-feet of water and 1.16 percent of the District supply. This use represented the greatest relative gain, 31.66 percent. Tables 9 and 10 summarize the changes in allotments for each contract class and major use between 1955 and 1964. These changes in use provide a first indication of the flexibility of NCWCD as a water-allocation organization.

THE TRANSFER PROCESS IN THE NCWCD

Transfers of water from use to use are playing an increasingly important part in activities of water users in the NCWCD. There are two types of water transfers to consider. First are transfers of a permanent nature which may occur within the irrigation sector or any of the other sectors. Second are transfers which are seasonal (temporary) in nature. These transfers may be thought of as water rentals and, if freely used, would obviously be of value in getting water to those uses having high demands.

Permanent transfers of NCWCD water are relatively easy to obtain.

TABLE 9. SUMMARY OF CHANGES IN NCWCD CONTRACTS BETWEEN 1958 AND 1964

(acre-feet)

Year	Class B	Class C	Class D	Section 25	Temporary use
1958	44,950	6,000	197,340	61,710	1,110
1964	45,976	6,000	188,451	71,563	—
Percent change	+2.28	0.00	−4.50	+15.96	—

Source: Official records of the NCWCD. These accounts may be found in the District office in Loveland, Colorado.

TABLE 10. SUMMARY OF CHANGES IN USE OF NCWCD WATER BETWEEN 1955 AND 1964

(acre-feet)

Year	Irrigation use	Domestic use	Manufacturing use
1955	262,050	44,905	3,000
1964	253,169	53,241	3,950
Percent change	−3.42	+18.56	+31.66

Source: Official records of the NCWCD.

There are no legal problems involved in this type of transfer because the water is supplemental to the natural stream flow. Two parties, in negotiating for a transfer, agree upon a price for a certain quantity of water. A petition for transfer is sent to the Conservancy District requesting a change in the water charge to the new user. The District is not involved with the price agreement between the negotiating parties, regardless of whether they are individuals or companies. The District may refuse water transfers if it determines that the amount of water to be transferred is in excess of that amount which may be beneficially used, and it does prohibit transfers to users outside the confines of the District. A summary of the yearly transfers on a permanent basis from 1958 to 1964 is found in table 11.

The total amount under the first column of table 11 shows the amount

TABLE 11. SUMMARY OF PERMANENT TRANSFERS, NCWCD, 1958-1964

(acre-feet)

Year	Class D	Class B	Section 25	Temporary use	Removal	Total
1958	1,920	150	72	0	12	2,142
1959	2,650	0	72	0	99	2,734
1960	1,136	0	128	92	0	1,145
1961	886	2,000	54	153	0	3,093
1962	448	378	3,416	516	0	4,603
1963	1,293	309	1,561	872	0	4,035
1964	2,236	2,612	505	950	0	6,303
Total	10,569	5,449	5,853	2,383	111	24,365

Source: Official records of the NCWCD.
Note: For definition of classes, see text.

of water which was transferred to irrigation uses. This amount is made up largely of transfers from one irrigator to another. The transfers to Class B, Municipal Contracts, consist of 3,612 acre-feet of water transferred from Section 25 Contracts and 1,837 acre-feet transferred from Class D. Transfers to Section 25 came from Class D. Transfers to Temporary Use Permits consist of 1,000 acre-feet transferred from Class D and 1,383 acre-feet from Section 25. The last column, Removal, consists of water which the District Board members felt no longer was being put to a beneficial use.

Total transfers to irrigation use (from 1958 to 1964) amounted to 11,269 acre-feet. This figure includes transfers within Class D and transfers to irrigation use in the Section 25 Contract class. Transfers to domestic use totaled 12,970 acre-feet including transfers to Class B, transfers to Section 25 Contracts (domestic use) and transfers to Temporary Use Permits which are for domestic uses. Total transfers to manufacturing use under Section 25 Contracts amounted to 115 acre-feet of water.

Section 25 Contracts can be separated by uses as follows:

1. East Larimer District .... 480 acre-feet
2. Fort Collins/Loveland Water District .... 1,375 acre-feet
3. Lefthand Water Supply .... 1,120 acre-feet
4. Little Thompson Valley .... 1,606 acre-feet
5. North Weld County Water District .... 1,242 acre-feet
6. Longs Peak Water Association .... 252 acre-feet

These six organizations in 1964 held contracts which amounted to 6,075 acre-feet. Two other units used water for domestic purposes, but the combined acre-footage of these amounted to only 80 acre-feet.

Great Western Sugar Company and Ideal Cement Company were the main users of District water for manufacturing purposes, and the District Board allotted them 2,700 and 875 acre-feet of water, respectively. The Loveland Development Company also used water for this purpose but only in the amount of 15 acre-feet.

Permanent transfers of Class D allotments must be granted by the Board of Directors of the NCWCD. A definite number of acre-foot units is allotted to a specific tract of land. The allotment is, by law, attached to that tract of land and thus the land is subject to the ad valorem levy mentioned earlier. The allotment follows the land when the land changes owners. When land is sold, the purchaser notifies the District of the change in allottees.

Another instance in which reallocation or transfer may take place is in the division of property ownership or in the case in which water is to be shifted to another tract of land. Only the Board of Directors has the power to authorize reallocations or transfers of District water supplies. Reallocation of water allotments refers to the process of dividing an allotment among certain described sections of land that lie within the boundaries of the land specified in the original petition and order for allotment.

Allotment transfer refers to the process by which the Board of Directors transfers original allotments to other lands lying within the District. Tax liens are removed from the lands from which water is being transferred and are created on those lands to which the allotment is being transferred.

The second aspect of water transfer is seasonal transfer or water rental. The need for this type of transfer arises from insufficient water supplies caused by changes in crop patterns, the acquisition of new lands to be put under irrigation, or simply from an over- or under-estimation of original water needs.

The excess water that may be rented to owners of land with insufficient supplies comes from lands that no longer need the total supply allotted to them and from various water companies that have excesses of water in storage. Rentals make possible a higher degree of flexibility in getting water to lands having the greatest and most urgent need.

Anderson's study, noted in chapter IV, cites three factors which make possible the rental of water in this area. First is company ownership of water; second, the development of privately owned storage reservoirs; and third, of primary interest here, the availability of supplementary water supplies from the Colorado-Big Thompson Project.[6]

In company ownership of water, water rights are not attached to a specified section of land. Water users own stock in the ditch company and receive water in accordance with the amount of stock owned. As personal property, stocks can be sold and rented at the stockholder's discretion. Privately owned storage reservoirs are also owned by stockholders. Here too, the amount of water received is determined by the amount of stock owned, and transfers take place through the sale or rent of shares. The Colorado-Big Thompson Project is the third factor permitting the transfer of water. The water delivered through project works is freely transferable to any area lying within the boundaries of the District.

For example, User A obtains his water from Handy Ditch. User B obtains his from Home Supply Ditch. User B finds that his water supply is insufficient to meet his needs, while User A has excess water temporarily available. The two individuals negotiate a satisfactory price for the water and notify the secretary of Handy Ditch that the transfer is to

[6] Raymond L. Anderson, "The Irrigation Water Rental Market: A Case Study," *Agricultural Economics Research,* June 1961.

take place. The order form is completed and sent to the NCWCD head-quarters in Loveland, and the accounts are credited with the transfer.

The NCWCD office keeps no record of transfers between individuals within the same ditch company. The water is simply diverted to the new user on the ditch. Generally, transfers of this type are found in the small ditch companies, and no records are kept of the transfers. The rental arrangement is between two individuals, the rentor and the rentee. The parties notify the company secretary, who keeps the water records, that changes in water deliveries are to be made.

A study of seasonal water rentals within the District for 1958 found that 512 transfers which involved a total of 94,707 acre-feet took place. Of the total amount, 490 transactions totaling 91,285 acre-feet were transferred to irrigation use. Eighteen contracts were rented to domestic uses, amounting to 2,447 acre-feet. There were four rentals to manu-facturing concerns which totalled 212 acre-feet. Domestic users rented 25,515 acre-feet to irrigation users. There were 398 transfers, including 66,609 acre-feet, among irrigation users. Eleven transfers came from manufacturing uses and amounted to 3,345 acre-feet.

The same kind of inquiry was undertaken for the year 1963, in which there is a total of 607 individual transfers amounting to 104,450 acre-feet. There were 598 individual transfers to irrigation use amounting to 102,930 acre-feet. Only six rental transactions were to domestic uses, and these accounted for 1,239 acre-feet. The three remaining transfers were to manufacturing uses and amounted to 280 acre-feet. The freedom with which transfers take place in the NCWCD is evident: 30.5 percent of the total water available in 1958 was involved in transfers of a sea-sonal nature, and this proportion grew by 1963 to 33.6 percent. Table 12 summarizes these transfers

TABLE 12. SEASONAL WATER TRANSFERS, NCWCD, 1958 AND 1963

Year	Transfers to given uses			Transfers from given uses		
	Number	Use	Acre-feet	Number	Use	Acre-feet
1958	490	Ir	91,285.3	398	Ir	66,609.7
	18	D	2,447.0	103	D	25,515.0
	4	M	212.0	11	M	3,345.6
Total	512		94,707.3	512		94,707.3a
1963	598	Ir	102,930.7	407	Ir	71,076.8
	6	D	1,239.6	132	D	30,108.5
	3	M	280.0	5	M	3,265.0
Total	607		104,450.3	607		104,450.3b

Source: Archives of the Northern Colorado Water Conservancy District, Loveland, Colo. 1958 and 1963.
Symbols: Ir, Irrigation; D, Domestic; M, Manufacturing.
a This figure is 30.55 percent of the total available allotment of District water.
b This figure is 33.69 percent of the total available allotment of District water.

The question which arises from the data obtained is, why do municipalities, even in years when city water is rationed, transfer or rent water to other uses? The answer lies in the limited city facilities for storage. Fort Collins, for example, has storage facilities which can keep only one day's supply of water at a time. The water that cannot be stored is available for rent to those having an immediate need for the water.

The price of rented water in dry years may reach as high as $30 per acre-foot. These prices are of concern to NCWCD officials and, for a time, the District considered placing maximum rates on water rentals. It abandoned this idea because NCWCD officials were unwilling to hinder the flexibility of water use. They decided to let the parties involved, whether irrigation companies, municipalities, or private persons, negotiate the terms of the transfers. They reasoned that if one party thought the value of the use to which the water would be put warranted a high price, all concerned would benefit. The party renting the water receives a price which is at least equal to the returns he gets by using the water. The party receiving the water gains from the use of the rented water an amount at least equal to the cost of the resource. This arrangement accords with economic efficiency criteria.

THE WITHIN-DISTRICT WATER MARKET

A statistical analysis of the value of irrigation water within the Conservancy District was published in 1960 for the years 1955-1960,[7] the first six years of operation of the Colorado-Big Thompson Project. Estimates were derived for both ditch company water and CBT water from observations of a total of 337 farm sales. The observations were classified and analyzed by ditch company area, by county, and by size of farm. It was hypothecated that, if an active water market existed, values of company-held rights and CBT contracts would not be statistically different for the above categories. Rigidities in the transfer from area to area, lack of information, and other market imperfections would result in a varying value of water.

Statistical results indicated significantly different values between ditch company areas and between size-of-farm categories for both company water and CBT water.[8] Company water values did not differ significantly between counties except for Morgan County, which is physically remote from the rest of the District.[9] However, CBT water values were signif-

---

[7] L. M. Hartman and R. L. Anderson, *Estimating Irrigation Water Values*, Agricultural Experiment Station, Colorado State University (U.S. Department of Agriculture Economic Research Service co-operating), Technical Bulletin 81, 1963.

[8] *Ibid.*, p. 20, table 6, and p. 23, table 7.

[9] *Ibid.*, p. 18, table 4.

icantly lower for Weld County, where it is well known that company-held decree rights are the oldest and constitute the best supply in the District. Lack of a standardized measure of water supply precludes any firm conclusion from the analysis of company water values. For example, the majority of the direct diversion decrees in the North Poudre Irrigation Company, which was used as an illustrative example in chapter IV, are very late in date. This means that their supply is highly variable and, as would be expected, the value of water on farms from that supply was low in the statistical estimates. As was indicated in chapter IV, the addition of CBT water to their supply has caused a striking increase in values of shares sold recently. However, the lag in the effect of this change in supply on buyers' and sellers' evaluations precluded its appearance during the period of the statistical analysis.

This analysis does point up one very firm conclusion: that an active market had not developed for CBT water in the six years from 1955 to 1960. This water is freely transferable within the District and, being stored water, the supply characteristics are stable and well known. Recent municipal and domestic district activity in buying project water contracts gives evidence that a well-developed market exists at the present time.[10] Speculative holding of contracts for anticipated municipal demand may hamper reallocations within irrigated agriculture. However, the fact that yearly rentals are easily negotiated does, to some extent, overcome this factor.

CONCLUSIONS

A nine-year average water delivery, 1953-1962, in the District indicates 506,000 acre-feet from direct diversion, 114 acre-feet from local storage, and 221 acre-feet from project storage. The fact that project water constitutes approximately 25 percent of total water use provides highly credible evidence that this area has solved its reallocation problems with a project of this size and with the transfer rules adopted by the District. One would have to find other sources of rigidity than those of a water market if the productivity of water at the margin were significantly different between uses within the District boundaries.

The criteria based on return flow, as developed in chapter II, are not being followed by the District transfer rules, since return flows are entirely ignored. If all the transfers of District water were to municipalities, this would create no problems for efficient use, since growing urban areas are near the head of the irrigated valleys and domestic consumptive use is lower than that of irrigated agriculture. Being upstream

[10] Anderson, "The Irrigation Water Rental Market."

from the main agricultural use permits re-use potential from returns to be exhausted. Some transfers to boundary-line District users may not be efficient, in terms of return flow re-use, for the maximum income to the District. However, from an overall welfare point of view, downstream users in Nebraska may have as high a value of the marginal product of water as District users.

APPENDIX TABLES FOR CHAPTER V

TABLE A-V-1. NORTHERN COLORADO WATER CONSERVANCY DISTRICT OPERATING COSTS, 1962, AND PROJECTIONS TO 2001

Year	Total fixed costs	Replacement fund	Total variable costs	Total costs
1962	$ 512,615	$ 30,500	$ 353,877	$ 896,992
1972	510,327	30,500	458,557	999,384
1982	558,039	30,500	563,327	1,151,776
1992	1,155,750	30,500	667,917	1,854,167
2001	1,145,775	30,500	762,128	1,938,403
Total[a]	$37,679,285	$1,189,400	$27,295,932	$66,468,817

Source: J. R. Barkley, J. C. Nelson, and John B. Clayton, *Special Report on Trends and Revenues and Operating Costs and Provisions for Potential Revenue Increase,* (Northern Colorado Water Conservancy District, 1962), p. 3.
[a] Totals were obtained by multiplying each figure of each column through 1992 by 10 and each figure in each column in the 2001 row by 9 and adding the results.

TABLE A-V-2. ANNUAL REVENUE ESTIMATES, NCWCD, BY CONTRACT CLASS FOR ACRE-FEET ALLOTTED

Contract class	Acre-feet	Revenue
B—(Municipal)	45,135	$ 74,322
C—(Irrigation districts)	6,000	9,000
Section 25—		
(Corporations)	62,132	98,358
(State lands)	905	1,810
D—(Private individuals)	195,648	297,175
Total	310,000	$481,175

Source: Barkley, Nelson, and Clayton, *Special Report on Trends . . . ,* p. 6.

TABLE A-V-3. EXPECTED REVENUES, NCWCD, 1962-2001

Year	Water use revenues	Ad valorem revenues	Interest income	Total revenue
1962	$481,175	$403,313	$15,000	$ 899,488
1972	481,175	517,385	15,000	1,013,560
1982	481,175	637,777	15,000	1,133,952
1992	481,175	809,636	15,000	1,305,811
2001	481,175	992,482	15,000	1,488,657

Source: Barkley, Nelson, and Clayton, *Special Report on Trends . . . ,* p. 8.

TABLE A-V-4. COMPARISON OF ANNUAL EXPECTED COSTS AND ANNUAL EXPECTED REVENUES, NCWCD, 1962-2001

Year	Total revenue	Total cost	Difference	
1962	$ 899,488	$ 896,992	$ 2,496	+R
1972	1,013,560	999,384	4,176	+R
1982	1,133,952	1,151,776	18,824	+C
1992	1,305,811	1,854,167	548,356	+C
2001	1,488,657	1,938,403	449,746	+C

Source: Barkley, Nelson, and Clayton, *Special Report on Trends . . .*

TABLE A-V-5. NCWCD WATER DELIVERIES, BY YEAR AND MONTH, AND MEAN ANNUAL PRECIPITATION, 1958-1963

Month	1958	1959	1960	1961	1962	1963
Water deliveries (acre-feet):						
April-June	15,833	9,167	5,708	664	19,035	92,217
July	81,133	58,983	46,481	39,465	101,983	64,755
August	107,694	96,404	100,647	57,450	84,935	62,049
September	62,693	47,670	51,141	34,338	53,837	45,237
October	20,711	20,769	8,634	477	23,111	34,024
Total	288,064	232,933	212,611	132,394	282,901	298,282
Mean annual precipitation (inches):	12.73	14.00	10.01	19.70	13.68	12.97

Source: Northern Colorado Water Conservancy District, *Annual Report of the Secretary-Manager for Fiscal Year 1962-1963,* p. 35.

CHAPTER VI

WATER ORGANIZATIONS: THE SOUTHEASTERN COLORADO WATER CONSERVANCY DISTRICT

The Southeastern Colorado Water Conservancy District (SCWCD) is located in the Arkansas Valley and serves as the development and management organization for the Fryingpan-Arkansas diversion project. By 1972, the project will deliver supplemental water from the watershed of the Fryingpan River to users in the Arkansas Valley on the eastern slope.

The Arkansas Valley extends for some 340 miles from Leadville, the headwaters of the Arkansas River in the high Rockies, to the Colorado-Kansas boundary. The area consists of 26,000 square miles, slightly more than the state of West Virginia, and encompasses 280,000 acres of irrigated land. The major portion of the irrigated lands is classed as of high to medium productivity. The main crops grown in the Valley are hay, fruits, vine and truck crops, alfalfa, sugar beets, and certain specialty crops. Industries included in the area activities are farming, ranching, mining, recreation, and manufacturing.[1] While the area as a whole is sparsely populated, it includes Colorado's second and third largest cities.

As far back as 1936, the U.S. Bureau of Reclamation initiated a study of the upper Arkansas River in order to appraise water needs and to determine possible solutions to water problems.[2] In 1946 the Water Development Association of Southeastern Colorado was organized to facilitate efforts of water users to get a project proposed. As a result of the association's efforts, a steering committee was appointed in the Bureau of Reclamation whose purpose was to coordinate project planning between the eastern and western slopes.

The project was deemed feasible both from an engineering and

[1] *The Fryingpan-Arkansas Project* (Southeastern Colorado Water Conservancy District, 1964), p. 2.

[2] *History of the Fryingpan-Arkansas Diversion Project* (Southeastern Colorado Water Conservancy District, 1964), p. 1.

economic viewpoint in 1948; and in 1949, negotiations between eastern and western slope water users began. Many of the same problems found in the development of the Colorado-Big Thompson Project existed for the Fryingpan-Arkansas Project. Western slope representatives were willing to aid eastern slope water users but not at their own expense. They would cooperate as long as the demands for water on the eastern slope were reasonable and western slope storage requirements were met.

In 1950, the two factions reached an agreement and set forth the principles of the project operation. These principles included maximum conservation and maximum use of water diverted from the western slope, a declaration of the protection afforded the western slope users, and the preservation of water used for recreation.[3]

The Aspen Reservoir being constructed by the Bureau of Reclamation for the purpose of storing replacement water for the western slope will have an active capacity of 28,000 acre-feet and must be completed before any water may be diverted to the eastern slope. Any of the reservoir capacity which is not needed for replacement purposes is excess or surplus capacity. This surplus capacity may be sold or leased by the Bureau to various western slope users, and charges for the use of this water will be comparable to charges made for project water on the eastern slope.

The project will consist of the construction of four reservoirs, various canals and tunnels, and certain power features in addition to the Aspen Reservoir. The major structures that will be included in the project are summarized in three appendix tables.

PROCEDURE FOR ALLOTMENT OF DISTRICT WATER

The SCWCD is still in its formative stage, and operating procedures have not yet been finally determined. In general, the prospective procedure for allotment of District water will be much like that in the Northern Colorado District. The SCWCD, which will be the contracting agency for project water, will develop individual contracts for petitioners, depending on the use to be made of the water.

However, the two Districts will be dissimilar in the priorities given to the various water uses. In SCWCD, domestic (municipal) use will have priority over any other use. Although the District has not yet allotted any water, it has obligated itself to divert 10,000 acre-feet to the Colorado Springs area through a 38-mile pipeline.[4] The District will

---

[3] *Operating Principles Governing Fryingpan-Arkansas Water Diversion Project* (Water Development Association of Southeastern Colorado, March, 1955), p. 3.

[4] *Fryingpan-Arkansas Background Information* (U.S. Department of the Interior, June 20, 1962), p. 10.

probably allot another 3,000 acre-feet of the 20,500 acre-feet currently expected to be available for domestic use and divide the remaining 7,500 acre-feet among towns such as Crowley, Rocky Ford, Las Animas, and Eads which are downstream on the Arkansas.

Another difference between the two conservancy districts will be in rates charged for water. NCWCD rates vary according to the type of use. But the SCWCD will set a flat rate for all uses. The rate now proposed is $5.40 per acre-foot, but this figure is neither a ceiling nor a floor on rates that may be charged, as will be explained later.

In addition to domestic and industrial water, the SCWCD will have about 163,000 acre-feet available for irrigation. As in the northern district, this water will be supplemental to existing water supplies; that is, it will be allotted to land already under irrigation and not to irrigate new land acreage. Thus, like its northern counterpart, SCWCD will not grant allotments according to existing decree priorities.

The 163,000 acre-feet is an estimate which includes wasted water, return flows, and winter storage, quantified as follows:

1. District water released at Pueblo Reservoir consists of western slope imports plus conservation of flood flows. This amounts to an expected 49,000 acre-feet.

2. Arkansas River winter storage is expected to amount to 65,900 acre-feet.

3. New water developed by the Twin Lakes Canal Company accounts for an expected 11,800 acre-feet.

4. Indirect water consisting of return flows and re-use from Twin Lakes water will be approximately 4,700 acre-feet.

5. Return flows from municipal and industrial water are expected to be 11,400 acre-feet.

6. Re-use from project imports is expected to be 19,800 acre-feet.[5]

TERMS OF THE REPAYMENT CONTRACT

Although the SCWCD is a new organization in which operating procedures are not entirely spelled out, the repayment contract with the United States identifies some of the major differences between the two conservancy districts. The contract with the United States for repayment of construction costs of the Colorado-Big Thompson Project is a fixed-payment contract, which requires the NCWCD to repay a fixed amount within the repayment period. The contract between the SCWCD and the United States is a water-service contract with provision for renewal and is flexible concerning charges for repayment by the District.

[5] Memorandum to Secretary of the Interior from Commissioner of Reclamation, Dec. 11, 1964, p. 3.

The reasons for the difference in the contracts are these: (1) the long period of construction for the Fryingpan-Arkansas Project during which construction costs might rise significantly; (2) large changes in the amount of anticipated supplemental water supplies which could cause great fluctuations in District revenues for repayment; and (3) the dependence on the long-run growth of ad valorem tax revenues enabling the District to meet its share of the construction costs.

SCWCD, in its capacity as the project repayment agent, has the responsibility to repay as follows:

1. The cost of project works allocated to irrigation and assigned to the District, currently estimated to be $53,568,744.

2. The cost of project works allocated to municipal and industrial uses—currently estimated to be $6,541,000—plus interest during and after construction at the rate of 3.046 percent per annum.

3. An appropriate share (currently estimated to be $107,000) of the annual costs of operation and maintenance of project works.[6]

The repayment period is 40 years and is now expected to begin in 1972. The annual service charge payable by the SCWCD consists of the following three parts:

1. An amount equal to the yield from a levy of nine-tenths of one mill on the assessed valuation of all taxable property within the District.

2. Five dollars and forty cents ($5.40) for each acre-foot of project water delivered to the District for irrigation and municipal and industrial use.

3. Two dollars and twenty-five cents ($2.25) for each acre-foot of winter-stored water delivered to the District.[7]

The collections from the property tax are estimated to be approximately $480,000 in 1972 and increase to $891,000 by 2029. Payments for project water, tentatively set at $5.40 per acre-foot, are expected to produce about $378,000 per year. The sum of this amount over the 40-year repayment period will approximate 32 percent of the total District obligation to the United States.

As noted, the rate proposed for municipal and industrial uses of District water is the same as that for irrigation uses. The District, however, contemplates large increases in the ad valorem revenues to be paid by these users and may apply these revenues as though they were charges on acre-feet of water used. If this procedure is followed, the charge for District water used for manufacturing and domestic purposes will approach $30 per acre-foot. The same method applied to irrigation uses would yield a rate of approximately $10 per acre-foot.

6 *Ibid.*
7 *Ibid.,* p. 5.

These two charges, together with the expected charge of $2.50 per acre-foot on winter-stored water, will constitute the total payments made by the District for project construction. The Board of Directors of the SCWCD and water users within the District have not yet agreed upon the winter storage program, and thus it does not constitute a sure source of revenue. Basically, the program would require an agreement between the District and 20 ditch companies that the ditch companies forgo winter irrigation and store their winter irrigation water in Pueblo Reservoir and an agreement on the manner in which the ditch companies would share the releases of winter-stored water. The winter storage would amount to an annual payment of $148,274 to the United States, approximately 10 percent of the total obligation.

Another area of dissimilarity between the two districts concerns the rights to project water. NCWCD owns the rights to irrigation, municipal, and industrial water uses during the repayment period. SCWCD is, in effect, renting project water from the Bureau of Reclamation until such time as repayment is completed. The repayment contract between SCWCD and the United States reads, "During the term of this contract and any renewal thereof and subject to the fulfillment of all obligations thereunder, the District shall have the first right to the available project water supply. Upon completion of payment of the amount of the reimbursable project costs assigned for ultimate return to the United States by the District and subject to payment by the District to the United States in its operation and maintenance of project works, the District thereafter shall have a permanent right to the available project water supply."[8]

USE OF RETURN FLOWS FROM DISTRICT WATER

Of special interest here are the stands taken by the two districts concerning the use to be made of return flows from District water. NCWCD has elected to follow the state law, which requires that return flows become a part of the stream flow and are to be appropriated according to existing river decree. This will not be the case in the SCWCD, where both the United States and the District are in agreement as to the use of return flows. ". . . the District reserves the right to the use of all waste, seepage and return flow water derived from water furnished to the District by the United States and such reservation of right to use of such water shall be for the use and benefit of the District and those claiming by, through or under the District."[9]

---

[8] Contract between the United States and the Southeastern Colorado Water Conservatory District (Contract No. 14-06-700-4715, 1965), p. 7, Art. 4.

[9] *Ibid.*, p. 10, Art. 9, Sec. (c).

SCWCD will measure, through equipment provided by the United States, not only stream flow at the various headgates but also flows at different points of diversion. The recording device for measuring flow at the headgates is a telemeter, which can convey the streamflows at any particular measuring station, at any period during the day, to the District headquarters. An additional installation, the analogue computer, will allow the District to receive measurements as to the amounts of water diverted at each diversion point and thus the measurement of return flows from the diversions. This device will make possible the sale of return flows, which the District plans to use as another source of District revenues. It will also allow members of the District to receive additional supplemental water supplies.

Reference to figure 1 in chapter II will help to clarify District policy. Assume that users (1), (2) and (4) are District water users and user (3) is using water appropriated according to a river decree. Assuming that the District can adequately measure return flows from District water uses, and assuming that it does obtain the legal right to these return flows, then the District may bypass (3) in favor of another downstream user. It may be decided that (3) be allowed to petition for water in the amount of the return from (1) and (2). Provision to the effect is being considered by the Board of Directors of the SCWCD. The charge for the return flow water will be the same as the charge set for direct supplies of District water.

TRANSFER OF WATER IN THE SCWCD

Another basic difference between the contracts and operations of the two districts is found in the positions taken on the transfer of water between or among uses. The contract between SCWCD and the United States specifically excludes the resale of District water on the part of any user save municipalities. ". . . water furnished to the District pursuant to this contract shall not be sold or otherwise disposed of outside the District, nor shall any water sold by the District be resold by the District's water users for any purpose except that municipalities may, within the area served by them, resell project water but not the return flows thereof."[10]

The use or transfer of water outside the District is forbidden by the contracts of both districts. The same holds true for the sale of return flows by member entities of the districts. However, where the contract between SCWCD and the United States excludes the resale of District water by any user except municipalities, NCWCD allows relatively free transfers on the part of users in transferring water either through per-

[10] *Ibid.,* p. 10, Art. 10.

manent sale of water or through the seasonal rental of water throughout the District. The process which has been proposed in the SCWCD concerning the transfer of water is that, in the event of permanent sale of water, it is the District itself that does the purchasing and then the selling of water. Seasonal rentals (temporary transfers) will not be allowed in the Southern District. If the District finds excess water on one property, it will withdraw this water from the individual and will reallocate it according to areas of need.

The reasoning behind this procedure for the transfer of water is that it will eliminate competition between various water users for any excess water. Prices in cases involving water transfers should be kept reasonably low because, with the District purchasing the water, other companies or individuals will feel that they will be able to obtain the water at lower rates than they would have had to pay when buying under circumstances where water would go to the highest bidder.

CONCLUSIONS

Several consequences result from the transfer procedure outlined above. The first is that it will eliminate the possibility of windfall gains accruing to the original holders of contracts. This may be a main reason for instituting such a procedure. However, the consequences of the procedure on economic efficiency are not desirable. Restricting the price of the water to a nominal basis eliminates the allocative function of the market. Essentially the District will have no procedure for reallocation except in a very restricted sense.

Consider the situation in which the marginal value product of water in the first use is just equal to its price; e.g., the prospective $5.40 per acre-foot charge on District water. Referring to the example in chapter II, let us suppose a domestic use whose marginal value product is much greater than the nominal price of the water, for example, $30. An efficient use of water would require that water be transferred from use (1) to use (3) because of this difference in value product of water. If the transfer negotiations were left to the two water users, a transfer would undoubtedly take place. However, if the District must purchase the water before any transfers occur, water user (1) will not sell to the District at a price of $5.40 per acre-foot. The District could remove a certain amount of water from user (1) if he were wasting it. However, the conditions above assume that water is being used efficiently in use (1), so there is no reason for removal. Thus, a transfer of water which would have taken place from a low-value to a high-value use will not take place when the District is a middle man. Thus user (3), who would have been relatively certain of obtaining water from user (1) had market negotiations been allowed, is left uncertain as to whether or not any water will be available for transfer.

A similar analysis applies in discussing seasonal water rentals. SCWCD will not allow transfers of this sort. If excess water is available for rent, the District will remove it from service in the particular use and sell it to another use. This method will not only prohibit water from moving to its temporarily highest use but will also increase the amount of water wasted. If an irrigator in the Northern District finds that he has a certain amount of water which he will not need during a particular month of the year, NCWCD allows him to rent this water to other users having need for the water and still allows him his diversion in the following year. However, in SCWCD, the water user will not advertise water for rent because the District will withdraw that amount from use. The user has no guarantee that the District will again allot him the same amount in the following year. Rather than risk losing part of his supply, the first user will over-irrigate or at least not have the same compulsion to use water as efficiently as he would if he could market his water supplies.

The sale of return flows under this procedure also eliminates the possibility of windfall gains to holders of original decrees. It is conjectural whether sale of return flow, in this case, has any implications for efficiency. The District can just oversell its original supply by the amount of the estimated cumulative return flow. There may be some problems if District water diversions are all grouped at one end of the basin or the other, so that the re-use potential is eliminated. The problems this entails for transfers would be negligible, since the source of water is storage and is supplemental to an existing supply. The dependence of any given diversion on a return flow is not critical when changes in use are for the supplemental source which is available on demand and rights are determined on a pro-rata basis rather than a priority system.

APPENDIX TABLES FOR CHAPTER VI

TABLE A-VI-1. PROJECT STRUCTURES, FRYINGPAN-ARKANSAS PROJECT, WITH ESTIMATED COST, CAPACITY, AND YEAR OF COMPLETION

Construction	Cost	Capacity in acre-feet	Completion year
Ruedi reservoir	$12,831,000	100,000	1968
Diversion tunnel	9,230,000		1968
Sugar Loaf reservoir	6,063,000	117,000	1969
Twin Lakes reservoir	8,311,000	260,000	1969
Pueblo reservoir	34,603,000	400,000	1974
Arkansas Valley pipeline	8,025,000		
Total	$79,063,000	877,000	

Source: Files of the Southeastern Colorado Water Conservancy District, Pueblo, Colo. Information unpublished but available to the public.

TABLE A-VI-2. POWER PLANT CONSTRUCTION, FRYINGPAN-ARKANSAS PROJECT, WITH CAPACITIES AND ESTIMATED COSTS

Power plant	Average head	Installed capacity	Estimated cost
	(feet)	(kilowatts)	
Elbert & Canal	515	10,600	$6,528,000
Otero	287	19,800	3,958,000
Wapaco	495	20,600	3,830,000
Princeton	278	14,400	3,090,000
Pancho	268	18,500	4,200,000
Salida	405	28,000	4,748,000
Pueblo	120	12,000	3,155,000
Transmission lines 400 miles			12,000,000
Total	2,368	123,900	$41,509,000

Source: Fryingpan-Arkansas Project data found in the District office in Pueblo, Colorado.
Note: Proceeds from power sales are returned to the federal treasury to repay costs of power facilities and to some extent other costs, too.

CHAPTER VII

REGIONAL ECONOMIC INTERDEPENDENCIES

In a specialized complex economy, like that of the United States, economic interdependencies are quite pervasive. Economic interdependency within a region depends upon the self-sufficiency of the region, i.e., the amount of imports. The interdependencies with which we are most concerned in this chapter are those that exist beyond those among sectors which are mutually dependent upon water supplies.

An analysis of interdependencies may be used for several purposes in the overall problem of the study. In the first place, they serve as a basis for specifying conditions for a national-income-increasing transfer, where the assumptions of the competitive model do not apply; viz, where there are immobilities, indivisibilities in factor services and overhead costs, unused capacity (unemployment), and diseconomies or economies of scale. The specification of national-income-increasing conditions serves as a basis for analyzing the economic implications resulting from a market solution to the transfer problem. Also, the analysis serves to provide insight into the complex of economic interests which influence a transfer negotiation when a district or regional organization exercises control over the water resource. Lastly, estimates from this type analysis provide alternative cost guidelines for regions contemplating developing outside sources of water supply.

THE PROBLEM

In order to formulate the problem as simply and explicitly as possible, we will consider a three-region model encompassing the national economy. Regions A and B are relatively small and accessible to each other in terms of a water transfer, and the third region is C, the "rest of the world." A and B may also be interpreted in some cases as different uses within the same region. We will assume that the transfer goes from A to B and releases resources from A, which may or may not move into employment in B or the "rest of the world" and may pull resources

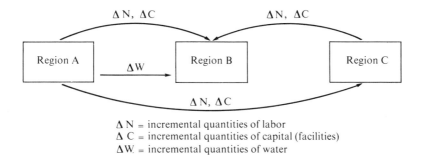

Δ N = incremental quantities of labor
Δ C = incremental quantities of capital (facilities)
Δ W = incremental quantities of water

Figure 3. Hypothetical resource movements among regions.

from the "rest of the world" into B. Possible resource movements are depicted in figure 3.

In figure 3, we have indicated a transfer of water from Region A to Region B. Depending upon the magnitude of the water transfer, possibilities of factor substitutions, demand elasticities, etc., there will be incremental quantities of labor and capital unemployed in Region A. Mobile labor and capital, denoted by ΔN and ΔC, may move into Region B or C as indicated. Also, it is presumed that the use of the transferred water in Region B will entail pulling other resources out of Region C or Region A, as indicated by the ΔN and ΔC coming into B. The diagram also is pertinent if A and B are interpreted as different uses within the same region. That is, movements of resources may be between uses rather than necessarily involving a spatial movement.

In terms of national income, it is obvious that the transfer of water into Region B increases income there in the basic use; otherwise the transfer would not take place. The transfer of water out of Region A decreases income there, other things equal. Whether the transfer affects the income in Region C depends upon mobility and the existing state of capital and labor employment. If labor and capital resources were perfectly mobile and the economy were in a state of full employment, then the simple criterion of the marginal value product of water in B being greater than that in A would assure a national-income-increasing transfer. A problem arises when in reality resources are not perfectly mobile and when less than full employment exists. Private sellers of water *do not* count as costs the loss of income to immobile labor and capital in secondary sectors, whereas it is a loss in national income. Also, buyers of water *do* count as costs employment of unemployed labor and capital, whereas it is not a cost to the community except for loss of leisure time enjoyment by labor.

We can pose the question—would the more or less free-market ideal of traditional economic theory necessarily operate to effect a national-income-increasing transfer under conditions of immobility and unemployment? The answer seems straightforward enough that it would not.

Without going into the details of the nature of immobilities and unemployment, criteria for national-income-increasing transfers can be specified under various sets of assumptions. They are derived from production function concepts and presented in the appendix but will be discussed briefly here on an intuitive basis. The existence of immobilities would appear to be a rather general phenomenon consistent with a normal state of economic affairs, whereas unemployment appears to be an aberration from a normal state of affairs. However, for symmetry of treatment the two have the same kinds of effects on transfer criteria except in the opposite direction; so we will consider both kinds of phenomena on an equal basis.

If we assume full employment equilibrium in A, B, and C and perfect mobility of all resources, then this implies that the transaction price for water must be equal to or greater than the marginal value product of water in its present use in area (or use) A to assure a national-income-increasing transfer. If there is a transfer cost for the resources, then the price must be enough greater so that the discounted value of the difference exceeds the transfer cost. In general, this kind of a criterion can be stated for any imperfections in the market process. If immobilities exist, then the transfer price of water must be enough greater than the present marginal value product of water to offset the loss of income due to the immobilities. On the other hand, if unemployment or underemployment exists in the buying area or use, then the transfer price could be correspondingly lower than the marginal value product of water in its present use, since the transfer would result in additional income to that attributable to water alone.

Under conditions of general unemployment the rather obvious procedure would be to compare the total decrease in area income in A to the total increase in B. Assessment of income effects for any one of the conditions regarding immobilities and unemployment involves economic interdependencies, since income in secondary sectors would also be affected by the water transfer. If we can conclude that the existence of immobile capital facilities is a general phenomenon, then the loss of income to these facilities is of the nature of an externality for a market solution, since the owners of the facilities would not be involved in the water-selling transaction.

There are very few a priori grounds for judging whether a free-market transfer would increase or decrease national income. It is obviously an empirical question for specific situations. An approach to measurement of the effects requires some understanding of the structure of a regional economy and some detailed analysis of the nature of the effects.

REGIONAL ECONOMIC STRUCTURE

The structure of a regional economy may be viewed as a flow of goods and services, expenditure payments, and income payments between sectors. Sectors are groups of economic units, where classification depends on the problem to be analyzed. For the water transfer problem

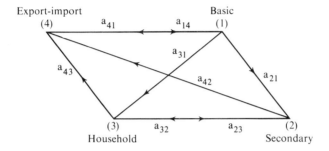

Note: In the figure $a_{ij} = x_{ij}/X_j$; i.e., the amount of the inter-sector transaction per dollar of output of the purchasing sector.

Figure 4. Flows of goods and services in a small area economy.

the sectors would be specified in terms of their interdependence with the basic water-using activity (sector). An illustrative flow table is presented in table 13 and a graphic counterpart to the table is presented in figure 4.

In the table, x_{ij} indicates the flow from sector i to j, so that rows represent the distribution of the sectors' output and columns the composition of inputs. In the household row (3), the magnitudes, x_{3j}, are income payments and the household column magnitudes, x_{i3}, are household expenditures on consumption. In an idealized model, the X_i row totals may be presumed equal to the column totals, i.e., expenditures on input purchases equal revenue from output sales.

TABLE 13. HYPOTHETICAL FLOW OF GOODS AND SERVICES IN A SMALL AREA ECONOMY

	Basic (1)	Secondary (2)	Household (3)	Export (4)	Total (5)
(1)	0	0	0	Y_1	X_1
(2)	x_{21}	0	x_{23}	0	X_2
(3)	x_{31}	x_{32}	0	0	X_3
(4)	x_{41}	x_{42}	x_{43}	0	X_4

In figure 4 a line between sector numbers indicates that a flow of commodities or services takes place between the sectors. The a_{ij}'s refer to the amount of the purchase per dollar of output of the purchasing sector. They are derived from table 13 by dividing x_{ij}, the column and row entries, by X_i, the row totals. For example, $a_{21} = \dfrac{x_{21}}{X_1}$, $a_{31} = \dfrac{x_{31}}{X_1}$ and so forth. An arrow pointing towards a sector number indicates a purchase from that sector. For example, the figure indicates that sector (1) purchases from sector (2). Arrows pointing both directions on the same line between two sectors indicate that both sectors purchase from each other, which results in a direct feedback, and consequent multiplier effects occur where a complete circle can be made between several sectors, following the direction of the arrows. Of the endogenous sectors (1), (2), and (3), the arrows indicate one-way purchase except between (2) and (3), the trade-service and household sectors. This means that the only multiplier relation existing in this model is between sectors (2) and (3), where rounds of purchases will take place. The multiplier relations from sector (1); viz.,

(1) → (4) → (1), (1) → (2) → (4) → (1), and (1) → (3) → (4) → (1), are leaked to the outside import-export sector (4). The sequence of transactions from an exogenous reduction of one dollar in the purchases of sector (4) from sector (1) is a reduction in purchases of (1) from dependent sector (2) amounting to a_{21} and a reduction of payments to household sector (3) of a_{31}. Both of these changes set off round-by-round or multiplier reactions between (2) and (3) which are equal to

$$1 + a_{23}a_{32} + (a_{23}a_{32})^2 + \ldots = \frac{1}{1 - a_{23}a_{32}}.$$

This multiplier relation is a regional consumption multiplier, estimated as one over one minus the regional household income generated by a dollar of consumption expenditure.

The income effects from an exogenous change in the basic sector can be estimated by adding together the direct effects and from this estimating the consumption multiplier effect. From figure 4 this would be $(a_{31} + a_{21}a_{32})/(1 - a_{23}a_{32})$, where $(a_{31} + a_{21}a_{32})$ is the direct income effect from a dollar change in basic sector output and $a_{23}a_{32}$ is the household income generated locally by a dollar of consumption expenditure.

To illustrate the income effects from a water transfer, suppose the basic sector is irrigated agriculture with a total water use of B acre-feet. Thus, the amount of gross output per acre foot is $X_1/B = b$ and the within-agriculture income per acre-foot is ba_{31}. For every acre-foot withdrawn, agriculture will reduce purchases from the secondary sector by ba_{21} and the secondary sector will reduce income payments to households by $ba_{21}a_{32}$. In the household sector, therefore, there will be $b(a_{31} + a_{21}a_{32})$ less income spent on consumption goods, immediately. As indicated above, there is a multiplier relation between the secondary and households sectors resulting from round-by-round changes in purchases and income payments. The total income effect for each acre-foot is, therefore, $\dfrac{b(a_{31} + a_{21}a_{32})}{1 - a_{23}a_{32}}$.

Let us look in more detail at the transfer transaction and the difference between the public and private economic interests affected. In table 14, the format of a more complex set of accounts is suggested with the household income row separated into proprietary and wage-and-salary income categories. Government has also been included where the government row (k) would be tax collections. Such a set of accounts, organized in an input-output matrix, is displayed merely to keep in mind the interdependencies. The following discussion will be directed towards hypothetical communities. In this discussion, some of the complications of regional accounts will be ignored. Hence the reader should keep in mind the descriptive purpose of the model and not think it is being proposed as an empirical model.

Let us assume that the only exports are from the basic sector, which is a water-using activity, and from the processing sector which uses raw material inputs from the basic sector. This would be typical of an economic community based on irrigated agriculture. Disregarding capital

TABLE 14. FORMAT OF A HYPOTHETICAL INPUT-OUTPUT FLOW TABLE

(1) Basic	(2) Processing	(3) Secondary	(4) ... Household supplying	(k) Government	(L) Household	(m) Export
(1) x_{11}	x_{12}	x_{13}	x_{14} ...	x_{1k}	x_{1L}	x_{1m}
(2) x_{21}	x_{22}	x_{23}	x_{24} ...	x_{2k}	x_{2L}	x_{2m}
.	.	.	.	.	.	.
.	.	.	.	.	.	.
.	.	.	.	.	.	.
(k) x_{k1}	x_{k2}	x_{k3}	x_{k4} ...	x_{kk}	x_{kL}	0
(L) x_{L1}	x_{L2}	x_{L3}	x_{L4} ...	x_{Lk}	x_{LL}	0
(m) x_{m1}	x_{m2}	x_{m3}	x_{m4} ...	x_{mk}	x_{mL}	0
						Income
R_1	R_2	R_3	R_4 ...	R_k	R_L	Proprietary
W_1	W_2	W_3	W_4 ...	W_k	W_L	Wages and salaries
N_1	N_2	N_3	N_4 ...	N_k	N_L	Employment
B_1						Water use

replacement and assuming that state and federal tax collections are offset by transfer payments in, then total regional income is equal to $\Sigma_j R_j + \Sigma_j W_j = Y$. In the proprietary income row, it is assumed that R_L represents rental income from all housing whether owned or rented.

If the processing sector is completely dependent upon the regionally supplied raw materials, then essentially it is also water-based, so the water input in the basic sector creates Y/B_1 dollars of income per acre-foot. In an extreme situation where there were no alternative uses for land and facilities, the sale and transfer of the water supply from the region would result in the total income loss of Y, with wages, ΣW_j, being partially replaced by labor movement. The resulting situation would be a ghost community with empty houses, store buildings, processing facilities, schools, churches, and so forth. And, of course, the relevant income calculation and the value of the water, in some sense, to that community is the total income as indicated.

Suppose the economic community were analogous to a company town; i.e., a community where a company owned and operated all of the economic facilities. If the company were negotiating a sale of its water supply, the relevant calculation of its value would be a capitalized value of the income flow in the proprietary income row, ΣR_j. In this calculation, the value of the water includes capitalization of income from all of the capital facilities of the community. The usual market calculation for a private transaction between sellers in the basic water-using sector and outside buyers would only consider capitalization of some portion of the income flow R_1. This example of an extreme case illustrates vividly the contrast between a private and a social calculation of income loss due to a transfer.

Further social losses would be involved owing to immobile labor and costs of labor movement; e.g., actual costs of moving a household and retraining. The human resource represents a capital investment in specialized skills in considering the social cost of change.

Types of Income Effects and Externalities

Several different kinds of interdependency effects have already been alluded to above. In this section they will be more specifically identified and the nature of the effect analyzed. The types of effects are: (1) a household income consumption multiplier effect; (2) a business multiplier effect on suppliers of production inputs and related sectors; (3) a cost-increasing effect on firms processing output from the water-using activity; and (4) an accumulative effect on the public sector through loss of tax revenues and reduction in use of public facilities. Effects (2) and (3) would be peculiar to the kind of water-using activity, and effects (1) and (4) would be general for any use. For an intraregional transfer, effects (1) and (4) would be matched by compensating effects

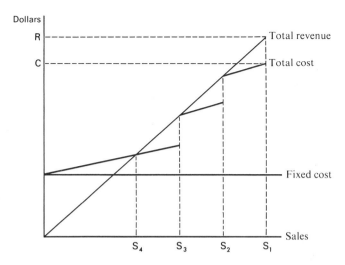

Figure 5. Cost-revenue relations for a trade firm.

stemming from the buying use; so effects (2) and (3) would be the ones of major concern. There may be some compensating results for type (2) and (3) effects also, depending on the nature of the changed uses.

The effect on profits of a decline in sales for a trade firm (wholesale or retail) is depicted in figure 5. This effect would stem from a decline in household income consumption and from a decline in demand for production inputs from the water-using sector, type (1) and (2) effects. Point S_1 represents some local equilibrium level of sales and corresponding profits of $R - C$. Some costs are perfectly variable as indicated by the slope of the total cost function; some are discretely variable as indicated at sales of S_2 and S_3, and some are fixed for all levels of sales. Thus, as sales volume declines, the firm will experience profits falling and going to zero at point S_2, thereupon it will release from employment a discretely variable input, a clerical employee for example, and move to sales volume S_3 and so forth. At sales less than S_4 the firm will be out of business, and the income effect would be $R - C$. However, any reduction in sales would result in a loss of profit income as indicated. In a multi-firm sector one would expect all firms to experience some reduction in sales as demand declined, and marginal firms would go out of business.

This loss of profit income is an externality if there is no compensating re-employment of the capital facility and if the market does not provide a mechanism for the profits, which are of the nature of economic rents, to be capitalized into the value of water. If this were possible, it would assure that the income of the new use would be sufficiently high to balance this loss. It would appear to be implausible that profits would be transferred to the water-using activity via a lower price on the input sales because of lack of incentives. This would be true inasmuch as demand for variable inputs is inelastic due to a lack of substitutability of them for capital and labor in the basic water-using sector.

The household income consumption multiplier effect is a community or trade center oriented effect and, in the context of water transfer, results from the loss of income payments to households and the subsequent reduction in purchases from household supplying sectors. The nature of this effect was explained in terms of the input-output model in the discussion of figure 4. A portion of that figure is reproduced below to facilitate the discussion of this section. The transfer induced effect originates in (1) and for every dollar reduction in gross output of (1) income payments are reduced to (3) (households) by an amount a_{31}. For every dollar reduction in income payments to households they reduce purchases from (2) and (4) by a_{23} and a_{43}, respectively. The reduction in purchases from (2) of one dollar results in a further reduction in income payments of a_{32}, and hence the multiplier effect between (2) and (3), as previously discussed.

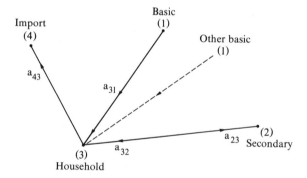

This brings us to an important juncture in the discussion, where we can specify conditions under which an income effect constitutes an externality. Generally, an externality, in the present context, occurs if factors of production are not mobile and able to replace the income losses due to the decline in purchases by the basic water-using sector. In the above example, if there are nonwater-based industries in the area which are growing, so that the negative income effect from the decline of the basic sector (1) is offset by a positive income effect, then household purchases from (2) and (4) will not be altered and no externality occurs. Since the nature of household consumption expenditures is independent of the source of income, the fact that sector (1) income payments are replaced by other sectors is irrelevant to sectors (2) and

(4) which supply households. Total area income is less than it would have been without the transfer; so potential economies of scale may have been forgone. The externality due to immobility occurs if the area is not growing, and the transfer results in an absolute decline in household income. Thus, some capital facilities and labor are unemployed in secondary sector (2), and the degree of immobility of these factors constitutes the externality. The decline in household purchases from the outside sector (4) will most likely not result in an externality, since (4) will be supplying other areas, many of which will be growing. Households supply themselves with housing and the loss of rental income would be an externality in a declining area, as indicated in the discussion of table 14.

The importance of the household income-consumption effect, as we have analyzed the problem, depends upon (a) whether the area is growing or declining in non-water-based industry and (b) the degree to which consumption goods are imported. An input-output model with household endogenous would reflect (b) and would estimate the local multiplier income effect. However, determining whether the effect resulted in an externality would involve investigating the state of the area's economy in terms of the condition under (a).

The effect on suppliers of inputs to the basic sector is depicted in figure 4 as a one-way purchase relation, as indicated below.

$$(1) \xrightarrow{\quad a_{21} \quad} (2)$$

In this type of relationship there would be no multiplier effect. For every dollar of reduction in gross output in sector (1) there would be a decline in purchases of a_{21} from (2) and the income effect is $a_{21}a_{32}$, as indicated. However, if (2) also sells to (1), then a multiplier effect occurs. A more circuitous multiplier would result if, for example, (2) purchases inputs from another sector which buys from (1). The existence of an externality for this effect would depend on the same conditions as that for the type (1) effect, except that the type (2) firms would be more specialized to the basic sector. Therefore, the presence of other growing sectors would not, in most cases, provide an alternative market for their output as would be the case with household supplying firms.

The nature of a type (3) effect is more complex than the previous two. The dependence of these types of firms on a water-using sector is depicted in figure 6. It is assumed that raw material production is land based, where (a) output is dependent upon water; e.g., irrigated agriculture. The location of processing facilities depends upon the relative magnitudes of the transport costs. If, for example, $C_I > C_F$, then the

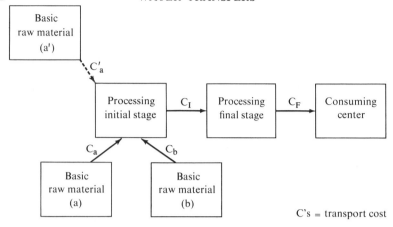

Figure 6. Spatial supply relationships for processing firms.

two stages of processing will be located together, if economies of scale are achieved by the final stage processing plants from the output of the initial stage processing plants. Also, if C_a or C_b is greater than C_F, then the processing will be located near the source of raw material production. In the figure an alternative source of raw materials (a) is indicated by (a′), so the externality effect of reducing the water supply at location (a) may be the increase in cost, $C'_a - C_a$, of buying from the more distant source or of bidding up prices at (a) to continue production at a higher cost due to the reduced water supply.

The relationships of figure 6 were developed with the meat-processing industry in mind. The initial processing stage for meat would be converting range animals, raw material (b), to fat animals using feed and forage, raw material (a), from irrigated agriculture. It is generally recognized that locational advantages are gained by locating the feed-yards and packing plants near the feed-forage supply, other things equal.[1] That is, the processing complex is production-oriented rather than consumption-oriented because of transportation costs. Since the meat-packing industry is also highly competitive, one would suppose that relatively small changes in input costs would cause a plant to lose its original locational advantage and it would be forced out of business.

The input-output model is not as amenable for manipulation to provide estimates of this effect, as for the type (1) and (2) effects.

[1] This conclusion was affirmed by Professor David Seckler at Colorado State University who is part owner of a vertically integrated irrigated cropland-feed-yard-packing plant operation located at Sterling and Wray, Colorado. Hugh Winn, livestock marketing specialist at Colorado State University, also affirmed this conclusion and provided additional information on the competitiveness of this industry.

With the (1) and (2) effects, we could start with the basic water-using sector and estimate the reduction in its output from withdrawal of water and, hence, reduction in input purchases or income payments, and the mechanism of the model gives these estimates. However, the type (3) effect is cost-increasing and, for incremental withdrawals of water supply, may or may not cause changes in output levels, depending on locational advantage, alternative sources of raw material supplies, and so forth. In the case where alternative raw material supplies are non-existent or economically infeasible and all the water supply is withdrawn, the input-output model provides an estimate of the total income effect. The rationale of using the model is to suppose that increasing costs price processing firms out of the market, so that total output of the final processing sector going to final demand is reduced to zero. Thus, the total income effect is direct income payments from the processing sectors and irrigated feed crops plus the indirect multiplier components for related sectors. The amount of the externality would depend upon immobilities of capital and labor. Illustrative estimates for a model and the nature of the calculations are presented in the following chapter. The remainder of the present discussion on these types of firms will focus on phasing out relationships due to incremental withdrawals of water supplies.

INCREMENTAL LOSSES OF SUPPLY AND PHASING OUT

In a situation where inter-use transfers are taking place within the same area—for example, from agriculture to municipal use or from any lower-valued use to a higher-valued use—the loss of supply for the established use would be by incremental changes. The incremental transfers would occur at a rate proportional to population growth or to the economic development of a higher-valued use. Thus, the entrepreneurs in the established use and their supporting or processing sectors would have opportunity to anticipate the decline in activity and phase out, to some extent, their capital facilities.

We can suppose that firms in type (3) category would be selling in a competitive national market and would be initially in a price-cost equilibrium as depicted in figure 7. That is, they would be producing at output Q with price P sufficient to cover average total cost given by the curve ATC_1. Initially, as water was sold from the basic water-using sector, these firms would bid up the price of the raw material output from the water-using activity until their cost curve was shifted to ATC_2 in figure 7, i.e., average total cost equals S while price equals P. In the figure $PT = SP$, so at ATC_2 the firms are not recovering their capital costs and income equal to these costs has been redistributed to the

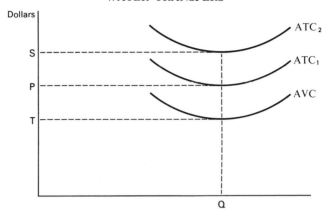

Figure 7. Price-cost relationship for processing firms.

water-using firms via the price mechanism. The higher price on the basic sector output would result in a greater return to water and a consequent higher price, reflecting the transferred profits from the processing sector. The type (3) firms would continue to operate until their capital facilities wore out or until water transfers reduced their supply of raw materials and increased their costs past a point on ATC_2.

The market could feasibly operate to phase out the type (3) firms as indicated if buying of water were not done immediately. However, if the entire basic water-using sector sold out at one time, the price would not cover the loss of income to capital in the type (3) firms. Thus, the existence of an external effect for this type of firm would depend upon a timing element.

Some aspects of the mechanism of local price adjustment are displayed in figure 8. It is supposed that processing firms will bid away their location and fixed plant rent to try to maintain level of output, giving the demand curve for processing crop inputs in the upper graph. Processing crops are competitive with each other and with export crops, giving the production iso-quant in the lower graph. Reduction in production of processed crop (b) resulting from the reduced water supply is partially recovered by an induced price increase in the short run. Toleration of reductions in output by the firms is influenced by the average cost curve, as pictured in figure 7. That is, if the curve is definitely U-shaped, then cost-saving incentives exist to maintain output near the economic capacity of the plant.

THE BUYING USE OR AREA

The kinds of interdependency effects discussed for the selling area (or use) apply, as has been indicated, to the buying area (or use).

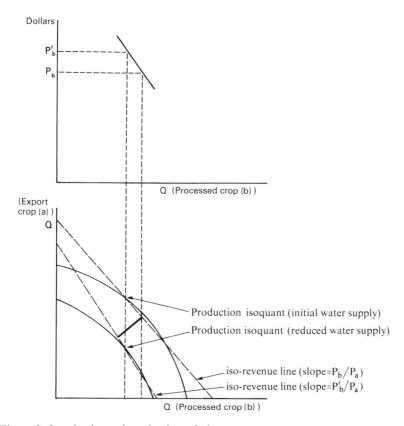

Figure 8. Local price and production relations.

Whether the transfer and consequent investment result in a marginal social product different from the marginal private product depends upon several factors. These factors are: (1) existence of unemployed labor and unused capacity and (2) external economies.

The importance of unemployment and unused capacity as an externality effect depends largely upon whether the regional economy is growing, static, or declining. In a growing region where the activity associated with a water transfer would add an increment to an already expanding economy, the existence of unemployment and unused capacity would be highly improbable. It is possible that one sector could be declining in an otherwise expanding economy, but these sectors would not be negotiating a purchase of water supplies. The likelihood of these kinds of externality benefits would thus be restricted to static or declining regions and, as pointed out above with respect to sectors, these regions would not be purchasing water supplies. At the time a transfer took place, some unused capacity might exist—for example, in the retail and public sectors—but to attribute any marginal social product externality to this effect would hardly be justified if other basic sectors were also growing. The most likely externality of any relevance would be related to economies of scale. Some of the effects related to the public sector will be discussed in the following section.

Public and Community Externalities

It is evident that externality effects from water transfers would not be confined to private market sectors or to purely economic effects. Since water transfers result in changes in levels of community income and population, the potential exists for social and political relationships being affected in a beneficial or adverse fashion and thereby relevant to the desirability of the transfer. We have made no attempt to analyze the nature of any of these non-economic effects. Two obvious effects of an economic nature which lie outside of the market decision process concern the public sector and the effects of market size on the public goods and services available to a community.

It appears that there are at least three kinds of externalities in the public sector. The first externality concerns the underutilization of public facilities in declining areas; the second concerns the economies and dis-economies of providing public services; and the third concerns the quality of public services, inasmuch as quality is affected by population variables.

With water and related population transfers, a stock of public capital goods will be underutilized in area A, the losing area, and duplicated in area B, the gaining area, after the transfer occurs. The loss of the value of these services in area A is, in some opportunity-cost sense, a regional income loss, although not subject to measurement in regional and national income accounts.

Certain public services have inelastic demands and require provision of minimal-type service. These minimal services are often associated with fixed investments in capital facilities. In areas of declining income and population and the resultant declining use, the per capita cost of pro-viding these minimal services may well increase, at least in the short run. Thus, inter-area resource transfers create for the declining area a declining tax base and an increasing unit cost of providing public services.

This characteristic of public sector behavior growing out of resource movements is illustrated by per capita expenditures on public services between five Colorado counties which have declined rapidly in recent

TABLE 15. PER CAPITA EXPENDITURES FOR PUBLIC SERVICES IN SELECTED COLORADO COUNTIES

	Five declining counties	Five growth counties
Per capita expenditures for education	$151	$138
Per capita expenditures for health/hospitals	23	4
Per capita expenditures for welfare	62	29
Total expenditures, per capita	$355	$247

years and five Colorado counties which have dominated Colorado growth.[2] This comparison is presented in table 15.

Table 15 suggests that cost economies are operative in the growth counties and/or that counties of declining population and declining or stable income suffer diseconomies in the provision of public services at the local level. The data are particularly significant in view of the expanding physical plants in the growth counties. Using education as a representative public service, suppose areas A and B before a transfer are both operating on the minimal range of a short-run average cost curve for educational services, point N in figure 9, where student population is measured on the horizontal axis and expenditures per student on the vertical. As the transfer of water resources is made between areas A and B, the declining population in area A has the effect of moving area A backward on the horizontal axis and to a higher point on the average cost curve—say, to point D. In fact, some data suggest that the average cost curve is not flat over an extended range and that diseconomies will exert themselves as population begins to increase beyond some point, R in figure 9. Variables other than population, such as quality of service, of course also affect the cost schedule.

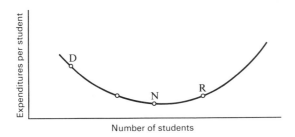

Figure 9. Average cost of educational services.

[2] This phenomenon, of course, is not peculiar to Colorado. Cf. Harvey Shapiro, "Measuring Local Government Output—A Comment," *National Tax Journal*, December 1961; and Henry J. Schmandt and G. Ross Stephens, "Measuring Municipal Output," *National Tax Journal*, December 1960.

The question of whether it will require an increase in expenditures to attain a minimal quality of public services in an area of economic decline introduces the quality question as the third kind of public sector externality. Virtually all legislative programs are based on the assumption that the quality variable in the provision of public services is not affected by the size of the service unit. For example, the Public School Foundation Act in Colorado provides for a minimal expenditure of $5,400 per classroom unit, irrespective of the number of classroom units in a school or district. On a priori grounds, there is reason to suspect the assumption that $5,400 per classroom unit provides a minimal quality of education regardless of student population.

Related to economic interdependencies are the effects of community size, or scale, upon the provision of so-called amenities of group life. We can assume as a basic fact that interdependence and mutual cooperation are a prerequisite for the provision of the amenities of social life and that this is only possible within some magnitude of population residing in geographic proximity. For example, specialization and exchange are basic to economic activity and result in certain benefits. However, these benefits are only achievable at some scale of production which is determined by the market; i.e., the magnitude of the consuming population. To illustrate this point, consider various sizes of communities and the kinds of activities performed. For example, one finds at very minimal levels of community size a one-room school, a general store, and a community church; at another level, a grade school with a teacher for each grade, a high school, a supermarket, other businesses, and several churches; and at another level a public library, an art gallery, a junior college; and so on at still other levels.

Assuming that the amenities of economic and social life are interdependently produced and are partially a function of population density and community income, we can further hypothesize that the function is of a certain form where amenities increase at an increasing rate, then increase at a decreasing rate and finally decline as population density increases. The last part of the above proposition implies some sort of an optimum geographic population distribution. The main point is that decisions concerning use of resources affect all of the community and this effect is not constant or linear with community size but depends upon the stage of development achieved by the community. Thus, some communities may value water resources more highly than others because of the different stages of growth which they exhibit.

Implications of Externalities for Water Allocation

A question posed by the preceding analysis of external income effects concerns the magnitudes of the marginal social product in both buying and selling areas (uses) involved in a water transfer. One possibility is presented in figure 10. In the figure, the marginal private and social product of water is arrayed as a supply schedule for the selling area and as a demand schedule for the buying area. In both areas, the social product schedules are higher than the private schedules owing to the income externalities. The intersection of the private and social schedules occurs

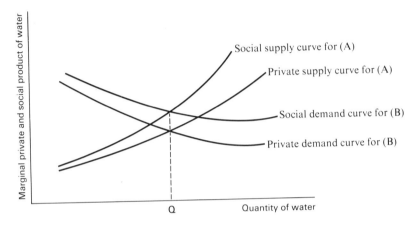

Figure 10. Public and private demand and supply relations for water in hypothetical regions A and B.

at the same quantity Q, indicating that a desirable transfer of Q from A to B for the private parties would also be desirable from a national welfare point of view, since income externalities are equal, by assumption, between the two areas. As indicated above, there appear to be no a priori grounds for judging whether this would be the case or not.

Income externalities in the selling area are minimized by timing resource transfers to allow phasing out of capital facilities. If area B were a growing area, income externalities due to excess capacity and unemployment would be minimal or nonexistent, and those effects due to external economies would be the only ones of significance. Empirical studies of specific instances would be needed to determine this question and to provide a basis for public action to either impede or subsidize a tranfer. It must be generally conceded that a purely private disposition of water resources is highly unrealistic, especially for a major inter-regional transfer.

CONCLUSIONS

Since most major transfers of water are, and presumably will be, carried out under the planning and direction of a public agency— federal, state or local—it appears that consideration of income interdependency effects can be most expeditiously taken into account in the planning stages when the agency is deciding on alternative sources of supply. Thus, the planning group can calculate the income effects of buying water from existing uses to compare with that of bringing in more distant supply sources. In arriving at a cost for buying out an existing use, the rate of withdrawal as it affects labor and capital mobility and the planning time necessary for recovery of capital expenditures is of critical importance. Specific studies would need to take into account alternative employment opportunities for land, labor, and capital facilities which would be different for types of use and area.

In chapter VIII, we present some illustrative estimates from an input-output study with an accompanying interpretation of the relevance of these estimates for the transfer problem.

APPENDIX TO CHAPTER VII

Derivation of Transfer Conditions

At the beginning of the chapter we discussed general considerations for transfer conditions that can increase national income in situations of immobility and unemployment. This argument is presented here in a systematic way, using regional production function concepts. Although some of these conditions seem quite obvious, a systematic derivation may help in clarifying the issues involved. The general model is as follows:

$$\text{Region A income:} \quad Y_a = f(N, C, W), \tag{1}$$
$$\text{Region B income:} \quad Y_b = g(N, C, W), \tag{2}$$
$$\text{Region C income:} \quad Y_c = h(N, C), \tag{3}$$

where N = units of labor, C = units of capital, W = units of water, and f, g, and h denote aggregate production functions for regions A, B, and C, respectively. Income and its change in the various regions are:

before transfer national income, $Y_1 = Y_a + Y_b + Y_c$; $\tag{4}$

after transfer national income, $Y_2 = Y_a - \Delta Y_a + Y_b + \Delta Y_b + Y_c + \Delta Y_c$. $\tag{5}$

The condition for $Y_2 > Y_1$ is that $\Delta Y_b - \Delta Y_a + \Delta Y_c > 0$ where

$$\Delta Y_a = f'(N)\Delta N_a + f'(C)\Delta C_a + f'(W)\Delta W,$$
$$\Delta Y_b = g'(N)\Delta N_b + g'(C)\Delta C_b + g'(W)\Delta W,$$
$$\Delta Y_c = h'(N)\Delta N'_a + h'(C)\Delta C'_a - h'(N)\Delta N'_b - h'(C)\Delta C'_b;$$

and thus the condition is

$$g'(N)\Delta N_b + g'(C)\Delta C_b + g'(W)\Delta W - f'(N)\Delta N_a - f'(C)\Delta C_a -$$
$$f'(W)\Delta W + h'(N)\Delta N'_a + h'(C)\Delta C_a - h'(N)\Delta N'_b - h'(C)\Delta C'_b > 0. \tag{6}$$

The meaning of symbols is: ΔN_a and ΔC_a are increments of labor and capital facilities unemployed in region A; ΔN_b and ΔC_b are increments of labor and capital newly employed in Region B; $\Delta N'_a$ and $\Delta C'_a$ are increments of labor and capital moving into employment in Region C, and $\Delta N'_b$ and $\Delta C'_b$ are increments of labor and capital which have left Region C to be employed in Region B. The notations $f'(N)$, $f'(C)$ and $f'(W)$ represent the marginal value product of labor, capital, and water, respectively. Thus, for example, $f'(N)\Delta N_a$ measures the change in regional income due to the change in the quantity of labor ΔN_a. The sum of the changes for all factors equals the total income change. This follows from a familiar mathematical theorem concerning homogeneous functions of degree one or that of production theory concerning constant returns to scale. The assumptions of constant returns is not necessary, but it simplifies the presentation.

Assuming that full employment equilibrium exists in Regions A, B, and C, and perfect mobility of all resources, the condition for a national-income-increasing transfer exists when

$$g'(W)\Delta W > f'(W)\Delta W, \tag{7}$$

where from equation (6) by assumption, $f'(N) = g'(N) = h'(N) = P_n =$ equilibrium wage rate; $f'(C) = g'(C) = h'(C) = P_c =$ equilibrium rate of return to capital; $\Delta N_a = \Delta N'_a$, $\Delta C_a = \Delta C'_a$, $\Delta N_b = \Delta N'_b$, and $\Delta C_b = \Delta C'_b$. Thus, all the components of income changes cancel out except the differential income change to water in the two regions. This is the traditional welfare economics solution for an efficient allocation of a resource, and it would be effected by a market system under the further assumption of profit-maximizing behavior by resource owners. However, if in fact resources are not perfectly mobile and full employment does not exist, then some alteration in the criteria is required. We shall examine relevant criteria under three sets of assumptions regarding mobility and employment.

These assumptions are listed below and spelled out in terms of the values of relevant variables. The condition (6) above is specified for each set of assumptions.

Assumptions (a) are: full employment equilibrium in A, B, and C, perfect mobility of labor, and immobility of capital facilities in A. This implies the values of variables and functions in (6) to be:

$$f'(N) = g'(N) = h'(N) = P_n = \text{wage rate};$$
$$f'(C) = h'(C) = g'(C) = P_c = \text{return to capital}:$$
$$\Delta C'_a = 0; \Delta N_b = \Delta N'_b; \Delta N_a = \Delta N'_a; \Delta C_b = \Delta C'_b. \tag{8}$$

And thus (6) reduces to

$$g'(W)\Delta W > f'(W)\Delta W + P_c\Delta C_a. \tag{9}$$

Under these assumptions the condition for a desirable transfer reduces to a question of whether the increased productivity of water (combined with other resources) in B offsets the loss of income from unemployed, immobile capital facilities in A.

Assumptions (b) are: unemployment in A, B, and C implying that $h' = 0$ for all factors. And thus condition (6) reads:

$$g'(N)\Delta N_b + g'(C)\Delta C_b + g'(W)\Delta W > f'(N)\Delta N_a + f'(C)\Delta C_a + f'(W)\Delta W. \tag{10}$$

Under these assumptions the condition for a national-income-increasing transfer becomes a question of whether the total income generated by the transfer of water into B is greater than the total loss of income in A; i.e., the left side of (10) is ΔY_b and the right side is ΔY_a.

Assumptions (c) are: full employment in A and C, unemployment or underemployment in B, and immobility of capital in A, implying that $\Delta N'_b = \Delta C'_b = \Delta C'_a = 0$. And, thus, condition (6) reads:

$$f'(N)\Delta N_b + f'(C)\Delta C_b + g'(W)\Delta W > P_c\Delta C_a + f'(W)\Delta W. \qquad (11)$$

The condition reads that total regional income in B resulting from the transfer be greater than the loss of income to capital and water in A.

It should be emphasized that the production function in this model includes both the water-using activity and related sector activities, so that employment effects consist of both a direct and indirect component. The unemployed capital in Region A, ΔC_a, may be looked upon as consisting of two components: one, which we will designate $\Delta_1 C_a$, is an unemployed increment of capital owned by the water user; and another component, $\Delta_2 C_a$, is an unemployed increment of capital belonging to suppliers of inputs to the water user.[1] Also, the marginal value product of water is one which takes into account consumptive use-return flow relations as developed in chapter II. The model is intended to indicate both the direct and indirect components of regional income changes due to the water transfer.

Suppose, for the moment, that the model exists under conditions where the buyers and sellers of water are also the users, i.e., that no organization or agency has control of water use. What would a free-market solution be under these conditions?

We can suppose that the transfer would not take place unless the following (free-market) condition holds:

$$g'(W)\Delta W > [f'(W)\Delta W + P_c\Delta_1 C_a]. \qquad (12)$$

This can be considered a free-market transfer criterion since the right side of the inequality represents the amount the seller would need to cover his loss of income and the left side the amount of income the buyer would earn in the new use. Under assumptions (a), the indirect effect on capital income, $P_c\Delta_2 C_a$, is not considered in the transfer and obviously would not be under free-market institutions. Thus, a free-market transfer could take place which would not be national income increasing if the indirect effect on capital income were of a sufficient magnitude. Condition (12) above is quite different from conditions (10) and (11), which were derived from sets of assumptions (b) and (c). Only with specific values of the variables would the transfer be national income increasing. The question this analysis raises concerns mobility and employment assumptions which are questions for empirical determination in specific situations.

---

[1] The component of income $P_c\Delta_2 C_a$ in secondary sectors may be an incremental loss due to an indivisibility and not necessarily due to abandonment of a sunk-capital facility.

CHAPTER VIII

ESTIMATES OF INCOME EFFECTS FROM
WATER TRANSFERS

The study estimates to be presented in this chapter will give some empirical content to the theoretical analysis of chapter VII, where the discussion concerned the nature of income effects from water transfers and was partially oriented around the input-output model. The analysis to be presented here is based on an input-output type of study. The Imperial Valley in Southern California was chosen to illustrate transfer externalities because of that valley's location near a large metropolitan complex and one that periodically experiences problems in providing water to its rapidly growing urban population. Also, an input-output model with related data for making income estimates was available for California.

The format for presenting and interpreting an input-output study is varied, depending on the interest of the investigator and his audience. The interest in this chapter is to throw light on the magnitude of the income externality resulting from a transfer of water out of agriculture. The burden of our presentation is to elucidate the economic interdependencies associated with irrigation water use. Economic interdependency is not necessarily contained within the boundaries of a geographic region but is related to the flow of goods wherever they may go. The well-defined regional containment of our interpretation of the study presented here pertains mainly to water use, which is geographically defined. Most of the presentation is developed in terms of coefficient or multiplier relationships, thus avoiding as much as possible the task of estimating totals for the regions used. We start with the usual multiplier relations and convert these to a per-acre-foot basis. The per-acre-foot estimates are then used to develop an economic base type of analysis which is presented as a supply schedule for water. Lastly the estimates are used to develop some illustrative capitalized values of the externalities on a per-acre-foot basis.

94

MECHANICS OF THE INPUT-OUTPUT MODEL

It will facilitate the explanation and interpretation of the empirical model to present an introduction to some mathematics on the technique itself and relate this to the estimates of income externalities. (Those readers not interested in such familiarity with the model may skip this section and proceed with the presentation of data.)

The initial tableau in developing the model consists of flows, as discussed in the previous chapter. A flow table for a two-sector model is presented below. Final demand is most specifically defined as the exogenously determined, or outside, variable affecting the system under study.

	(1)	(2)	Final demand	Total
(1)	x_{11}	x_{12}	Y_1	X_1
(2)	x_{21}	x_{22}	Y_2	X_2

In regional studies final demand would be designed to include exports. In the above set of accounts, it is obvious that if the total output of sector (1), X_1, is known and, also, intrasector use x_{11} and intersector use x_{12}, then $Y_1 = X_1 - x_{11} - x_{12}$, a residual. Thus, the components of Y_1 need not be derived explicitly.

Given the x_{ij}'s and the X_i's, the manipulation of these data proceeds by deriving coefficients, referred to in chapter VII, where $a_{ij} = \dfrac{x_{ij}}{X_i}$. It will be observed that $x_{ij} = a_{ij}X_i$, so the basic set of equations of the model can be stated from the previous table, as set out below.

$$X_1 - a_{11}X_1 - a_{12}X_2 = Y_1$$
$$X_2 - a_{21}X_1 - a_{22}X_2 = Y_2$$

This statement of the set of accounts indicates that total sector output minus intersector shipments equals final demand.

The matrix multiplication form of the equations, which is implicit in most tabular presentations, is as follows:

$$\begin{pmatrix} 1 - a_{11} & -a_{12} \\ -a_{21} & 1 - a_{22} \end{pmatrix} \begin{pmatrix} X_1 \\ X_2 \end{pmatrix} = \begin{pmatrix} Y_1 \\ Y_2 \end{pmatrix}$$

And in matrix notation we denote this multiplication as $(I - A) X = Y$, where $(I - A)$ represents the $(1 - a_{11})$, $-a_{12}$, etc. matrix, X represents the output column vector, and Y the final demand column vector.

The solution involves deriving a system of equations where the X's are functions of the Y's; i.e., the X's become weighted sums of Y's. The set of coefficients consistent with this statement is derived, for a large matrix, by the process known as inversion and the inverse coefficient matrix is denoted as $(I - A)^{-1}$. Thus the solution statement is $X = (I - A)^{-1}Y$ and the total output levels, X's, can be determined for any level of Y's. The form of the solution equations for the two-sector example is set out below.

$$X_1 = C_{11}Y_1 + C_{12}Y_2$$
$$X_2 = C_{21}Y_1 + C_{22}Y_2$$

The C's are the inverse or interdependency coefficients. The diagonal C_{ij}'s, $i = j$, will be equal to or greater than one and all other C_{ij}'s will be less than one. In our example, the C_{11} indicates the amount of increase in total output of sector (1) necessary to increase deliveries to final demand by one dollar. The coefficient will be greater than one by the amount of own inputs used in the production process of sector (1) and the amount of sector (1) output used by sector (2) to produce its output, which is used by sector (1) as an input. The C_{21} coefficient represents the increase in output of sector (2) for every dollar increase in deliveries to final demand of sector (1).

As was indicated in chapter VII, households may be included in the inter-industry transactions. In the flow table the row entries are income payments, and the column entries are local household expenditures. The coefficients are income per dollar of sector output and local expenditure per dollar of income, for household row and column respectively. In the inverse matrix, the household row entries measure the direct and indirect effect on regional income per dollar of change in sector j deliveries to final demand. Thus, $\sum_{j=1}^{n} C_{hj}Y_j$ (h = household row) is the total regional income of the industries included in the model, and $C_{hj}\Delta Y_j$ is the income change estimated from increasing or decreasing the jth sector's output to final demand by ΔY_j.

Where households are not included in the matrix, income effects per dollar of deliveries to final demand can be estimated by calculating the income per dollar of output for each sector, a_j, and multiplying the columns of the inverse matrix times this income coefficient row. For the kth sector this calculation would be $\sum_{j=1}^{n} C_{jk}a_j = M_k$, the resulting sum being almost equivalent to C_{hk} where households were included in the matrix. The difference between the two income multipliers, C_{hk} and M_k, is the income consumption multiplier effect, discussed with reference to sectors (2) and (3) in figure 2 of chapter VII. The study to be presented in this chapter, for California, does not have households included; so the above type of calculation was made to arrive at income multipliers.

If water use per dollar of output is calculated by sectors, water multipliers may also be calculated. For example, if water use per dollar of output by sector j is designated b_j, then $\sum_{j=1}^{n} C_{jk} b_j$ is the water multiplier effect of changing sector k's deliveries to final demand by one dollar.

ESTIMATES FOR SOUTHERN CALIFORNIA

Two basic California studies, an input-output study by Martin and Carter and a resource requirements study by Zusman and Hoch,[1] were used to derive the estimates presented in this section. Appendix tables A-VIII-1 and A-VIII-2 present the original coefficient and inverse matrices from the Martin and Carter model.[2] In our table, we have divided their household income coefficients into factor share coefficients and also added sector water requirements. Rental income for crops is the percentage share paid to landlords as reported in Extension Circular 104.[3] Labor income by sectors was reported in the Zusman and Hoch study and included income to management, family, and hired labor.[4] These estimates were used for the wage row of appendix table A-VIII-3. Rent and/or wages were then subtracted from the household income row of the model to get profits as a residual. Water requirements as presented in appendix table A-VIII-3 were derived as consumptive use requirements plus a delivery loss factor.[5]

MULTIPLIER ESTIMATES

Since households are not included in this model, the income multiplier coefficients are not estimated by the inversion process but must be calculated separately as explained earlier. Household row 37 in appendix table A-VIII-1 lists the income payments per dollar of gross output by sectors. Appendix table A-VIII-1 is the coefficient matrix

---

[1] William E. Martin and Harold O. Carter, *A California Interindustry Analysis Emphasizing Agriculture,* Giannini Foundation Research Report No. 250, University of California, Berkeley, 1962, pts. I and II, and Pinhas Zusman and Irving Hoch, *Resource and Capital Requirement Matrices for the California Economy,* Giannini Foundation Report No. 284, University of California, Berkeley, 1965.

[2] Martin and Carter, *A California Interindustry Analysis* . . . , appendix table II-1 and table III-1.

[3] *Guide Lines to Production Costs and Practices, Imperial County Corps,* University of California, Agricultural Extension Service Circular 104.

[4] Zusman and Hoch, *Resource and Capital Requirements* . . . , table VI.

[5] *Ibid.*

referred to above, and table A-VIII-2 is the inverse or interdependency matrix. The coefficients in the inverse matrix are output multipliers in that each entry C_{ij} measures the direct and indirect output required from the ith sector by a change of the jth sector's deliveries to final demand of one dollar. The sum of the entries in one column measures the total change in regional output required by a change of one dollar in that sector's deliveries to final demand. Multiplying each column entry by corresponding sector income coefficients (or by water use coefficients) and adding the products result in the regional income multiplier (or the regional water multiplier) as indicated in the previous section.

In the previous section, the calculation of the income multiplier was referred to symbolically as the sum $\sum\limits_{j=1}^{n} C_{jk}a_j = M_k$ for the kth sector. A sample calculation for meat animals from the tables would be:

$$1.000296 \times .162449 + .000079 \times .143573 \ldots$$
$$+ .024425 \times .551452 = .495865.$$

The direct income payments per dollar of output are the first product in the sum, approximately $0.16, and the indirect are the remainder, $0.33. Thus, in the production of meat animals, 16 cents is paid directly to labor and capital employed in that sector, and 33 cents is paid by sectors directly and indirectly providing intermediate inputs to meat animals. The household income row has been broken down into wages, rents, and profits (see table A-VIII-3). Further analysis is in terms of these categories rather than aggregate income.

The sum $\sum\limits_{j=1}^{n} C_{jk}\bar{b}_j = \bar{b}_j$ measures the change in consumptive water use in acre-feet resulting from a dollar change in the kth sector's deliveries to final demand. A sample calculation for meat animals from the tables would be: $1.00026 \times 0 + \ldots + .059559$ (grain) $\times .0233 + .000003$ (vegetables) $\times .0084 + \ldots = .013965$. It will be noted that meat animals affect water use mainly through the grain and forage sectors.

The income and water use multipliers broken down into direct and indirect effects for the 15 agricultural and related sectors are presented in table 16. It will be noted from the table that all the sectors affect rents and water use indirectly, which means that they purchase inputs from crops sectors or from other sectors which directly or indirectly use crops inputs. Thus, meat-processing affects rents indirectly because this sector purchases from meat animals, which use feed and forage crops.

The income multipliers estimate the backward linkage effects resulting from changes in output. The indirect multipliers estimate the increase or decrease in income payments to households resulting from an increase

TABLE 16. DIRECT AND INDIRECT LAND, LABOR, AND CAPITAL INCOME AND WATER USE PER DOLLAR CHANGE IN DELIVERIES TO FINAL DEMAND
(income and water multipliers)

Sector	Water Use		Wages		Rents		Capital	
	Direct	Indirect	Direct	Indirect	Direct	Indirect	Direct	Indirect
Meat animals		.0140	.0870	.1895		.0865	.0754	.0601
Poultry and eggs		.0056	.1530	.3047		.0609	.0094	.1570
Farm dairy products		.0126	.2830	.2071		.0958	.1267	.0753
Food and feed grains	.0233	.0013	.1610	.1557	.2500	.0227	.1585	.0489
Cotton	.0084	.0006	.2450	.1293	.2000	.0279	.2593	.0243
Vegetables	.0032	.0002	.3240	.1028	.0900	.0100	.3309	.0314
Fruit and nuts	.0077	.0002	.4930	.1386	.0900	.0105	.0431	.0514
Citrus	.0032	.0001	.3450	.1155	(.0900)	.0069	.2607	.0394
Forage	.0467	.0003	.3060	.1374	.2500	.3753	.0732	.0369
Misc. agriculture	.0039	.0013	.5390	.1257	.2500	.0141	.1532	
Grain mill products		.0084	.0860	.2129		.0889	.1509	.1089
Meat and poultry processing		.0051	.0820	.1574		.0319	.1282	.0698
Dairy products		.0068	.1610	.3485		.0432	.0606	.1424
Canning, preserving, freezing		.0024	.1270	.3463		.0491	.0760	.1321
Misc. agric. processing		.0012	.1460	.2163		.0203	.1602	.1032

or decrease in input purchases by the changing sector. None of forage output goes to final demand. Thus it is not correct to suppose that the income effects of table 16 are relevant for estimating unlimited withdrawals of irrigation water from that sector, since all of the output of forage is an intermediate good to other production. This type of linkage has been referred to as a *forward* linkage. The term is descriptive if one views final demand as the end process, with production below or behind in a dependency sense.[6] The input-output model is backward-linked, since the transactions represented are ultimately dependent upon final demand which is exogenously determined. The logic of the model is based on the dependence of the livestock-crop complex upon the processing industry, which in turn is dependent upon purchasers of its final demand. Therefore, from table 16 we can say if final demand for processed meat increases by one dollar, the regional effect on wages will be $0.082 + $0.157, on rents $0.032 and on profits $0.128 + $0.070. All of the income effects on grains, forage, and meat animals sectors are included in the indirect income effects. If we multiply the above income multipliers by the shipments to final demand of meat-processing, the resulting product is total income dependent upon the sale of that output. The grain, forage, and meat animal multipliers are redundant because they are already included in the meat-processing multipliers.

The kind of a model needed for the water transfer problem is a forward-linked one; that is, one where the dependency relation is developed from the water resource-supply based production up to final demand. The nature of this relationship was discussed with reference to figure 5 in chapter VII. The input-output estimates presented here must be interpreted in terms of the relationships of that discussion. The input-output procedure is relevant to the problem in terms of comparative statistics, because the forward-linked externality is a cost-increasing one which could result in the final demand shipments being priced out of the market. Certainly the input-output model gives no explanation of that process but presents only the interdependency of the backward linkage.

TOTAL OUTPUT AND FINAL DEMAND BY SECTORS

Using the notation of the previous section, the method of estimating sector total output and final demand will be briefly presented in symbolic form. The estimation of total output, final demand, and water use is used only to indicate relative magnitudes; their precise specification is not necessary for the purposes of our presentation, which uses pri-

[6] See Albert Hirschman, *The Strategy of Economic Development* (Yale University Press, 1961).

marily coefficient relationships. However, we present totals here to give a geographic situs for the study presentation. The Martin and Carter model was developed for California and our use of it is to illustrate the income based on irrigated water use in the Imperial Valley. The first step in the procedure of adapting the model to Imperial Valley was to arrive at output and final demand levels consistent with Imperial County census data. From this, water use by agricultural crop sector was derived using the Zusman-Hoch coefficients. To explain this procedure, we start with the coefficient statement of the model: $(I - A) X = Y$, where a typical equation multiplied out would be: $-a_{i1}X_1 - a_{i2}X_2 \ldots + (1 - a_{ii}) X_i \ldots - a_{in}X_n = Y_i$. (The $(I - A)$ matrix is presented as appendix table A-VIII-2.) Most of the total outputs, the X's, were available from Imperial County census data, so the Y's were estimated residually, as indicated above. In the case of agricultural processing, it was immaterial whether the plants were located in Imperial County or not, since the interest of our analysis was to derive the income, any income, which is partially dependent on Imperial Valley irrigated agri-culture. Of course, the dependency of a processing plant which uses Imperial Valley crops would decrease with distance from the Valley, since the plants could buy from other irrigated areas. It was assumed that the same proportion of crops was processed in Imperial Valley as in California as a whole. The method used for deriving the output of processing plants for meat and poultry processing will illustrate the rationale.

It was assumed that forage crops (sector 9) represented the most locally oriented irrigated crop input into the meat industry, in the sense that forage would be neither imported nor exported, so that $Y_9 = 0$. The census reports a clearly identified irrigated agriculture forage out-put figure. As will be noted in row 9 of appendix table A-VIII-2, meat animals and farm dairy, sectors 1 and 3, are prime users of forage inputs; so the output levels of these two sectors were adjusted consistent with forage production. Meat and dairy processing output levels were then adjusted consistent with meat animals and farm dairy. For example, it will be noted in row (1) of table 17 (meat animals) that almost all of meat animals go to processing, comprising \$0.30677 of the input cost to that sector. That row equation would read: $X_1 - .30677 X_{12} = Y_1$. Knowing X_1 and assuming $Y_1 = 0$ (as is true for the state), then $X_{12} = \dfrac{X_1}{.30677}$; i.e., the meat-processing level was assumed to operate at a level just sufficient to process the meat animals produced (fed) in the Valley. A similar procedure was followed for the other sectors, and results are presented in table 17.

TABLE 17. GROSS DOMESTIC OUTPUT AND EXPORTS FOR IRRIGATED AGRICULTURE, IMPERIAL COUNTY, CALIFORNIA

Sectors	Gross domestic output	Shipment to final demand and exports
	(000 dollars)	(000 dollars)
1. Meat animals	67,325.5	0
2. Poultry and eggs	26.2	0
3. Farm dairy	1,553.5	259.5
4. Food and feed grain	10,375.9	824.0
5. Cotton	28,100.2	25,875.2
6. Vegetables	32,962.9	20,976.6
7. Fruits and nuts	357.6	0
8. Citrus	1,027.7	60.8
9. Forage	19,077.1	0
10. Misc. agric.	18,509.2	4,107.0
11. Grain mill prod.	21,184.0	10,561.8
12. Meat process	219,465.5	207,727.9
13. Dairy process	2,580.5	1,214.6
14. Canning, preserving	87,866.6	85,213.7
15. Misc. agric. proc.	108,421.4	80,085.3

Source: Census of Agriculture estimates were used for crop outputs. Outputs for processing and livestock sectors and exports were calculated from crop output levels and appendix table A-VIII-2.

It will be noted that the major export sectors are cotton, vegetables, and the various agricultural processing sectors. The difference between gross output and the shipment to final demand is the use as intermediate goods. For example, the balance of meat animals, feed grains, and forage are inputs into processed meat, which goes mainly to final demand. The essential point, of course, is that the production of the final bill of goods requires the production of the goods in the total output column. We used the coefficient matrix to transform the raw material outputs of irrigated agriculture (known from census data) into the final bill of goods.

INCOME AND WATER USE

The income and water multipliers of table 16 give both the income and water use change per dollar change in deliveries to final demand. The reciprocal of the water multiplier for a sector is the value of deliveries to final demand dependent upon an acre-foot of water. This times the income multiplier for the same sector (m_i/b_i) gives the income multiplier per acre-foot of water applied directly and indirectly in producing the final output of sector C. These estimates are presented in table 18 by income categories and sectors. The total water use estimates are derived by multiplying shipments to final demand of table 17 by the water multipliers. The table array is shown graphically in figure 11.

TABLE 18. DIRECT AND INDIRECT INCOME EFFECTS AND WATER USE FOR MAJOR EXPORT SECTORS OF CALIFORNIA

Sector	Direct & indirect water use (acre-feet)	Dollars per acre-foot			
		Rent	Profits	Wages	Total
Food and feed	20,252	11.09	8.42	12.89	32.40
Cotton	232,308	25.38	31.56	41.68	98.62
Livestock group	1,073,592	6.29	38.61	46.95	91.85
Misc. agriculture	21,529	50.38	0	126.80	177.18
Citrus	203	28.96	89.79	137.65	256.40
Vegetables	71,761	29.24	105.94	124.76	259.94
Canning, preserving, misc. ag. process	297,418	18.95	152.26	250.21	421.42
Grain mill products	88,814	10.57	30.91	35.55	77.03

The array of water use and income categories per acre-foot in table 18 and figure 11 gives a picture of income relative to its water base. The income structure for this part of the California economy is derived in terms of dependence upon irrigation in this valley. In terms of totals the water supply of Imperial Valley, which is 1,805,877 acre-feet according to our requirement method of calculation,[7] supports a regional income of approximately 277 million dollars.[8] The income figure is the total area under the top income line in figure 11.

This analysis gives estimates of possible regional income losses for increments of water withdrawal, where the total income cost per acre-foot increases from $32 for food and feed grain to $421 for the canning-preserving industry group. What the analysis does not reveal is the income lost to the nation, as opposed to the region, since production lost to the region may be picked up elsewhere.

A Department of Water Resources survey of Los Angeles County, which contains the large metropolitan population of southern California, indicates a net water use of 1,073,000 acre-feet in 1960.[9] Estimates for 2020 indicate an excess of water requirements over approximate safe yield of local supply to be 1,975,000 acre-feet.[10] The annual rate of increase based on this projection is 32,900 acre-feet. With reference to figure 11, this rate of withdrawal would phase out the crops through export food and feed crops from left to right in the graph, and through

[7] The method for the coefficients of appendix table A-VIII-2 uses consumptive use requirement plus a delivery loss per acre per crop. Comparison with delivery estimates indicates that our method underestimates use.

[8] This estimate does not include the household income consumption multiplier effect.

[9] *Coastal Los Angeles County Land and Water Use Survey, 1960* (California Department of Water Resources, Bulletin No. 24-60, March 1964), table 12, p. 46.

[10] *Ibid.*

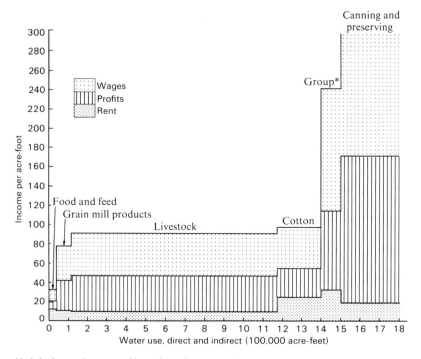

*Includes fruits and nuts, vegetables, and miscellaneous agriculture.

Figure 11. Calculated income to irrigated agriculture in southern California arrayed as a schedule of water use.

the feed and forage crops supporting the livestock industry in 30-plus years. Would this rate of withdrawal allow recovery of capital costs of fixed plant and induce phasing out?

ILLUSTRATIVE CAPITALIZED VALUES OF EXTERNALITY EFFECTS

It is quite obvious from figure 11 that income from water use falls into two quite different groupings. The livestock industry group and cotton, with a relatively insignificant export of feed grain, comprise a large block of water use with an income much less than the remaining miscellaneous, citrus, vegetables, and the canning and preserving industry group. Since the livestock industry group represents by far the largest single water-using group and also the lowest-valued major group, the following discussion will be limited to that group. Data for the meat-processing sector and its related sectors are presented in table 19. This table combines figures from the previous tables and from appendix table A-VIII-2. This grouping will be somewhat different than the live-

TABLE 19. MEAT-PROCESSING INCOME MULTIPLIERS AND ESTIMATES OF CAPITALIZED INCOME LOSSES, CALIFORNIA

Income Component:	Income multiplier	Income per acre-foot	Unrecoverable income	Capitalized income flow
Rent	$.032	$ 6.27	$6.27	$125.40[a]
Wages	.239	46.86		
Direct profits	.128	25.60	6.40	79.74[b]
Indirect profits	.070	13.72	5.36	66.79
Total				$271.93
Components of indirect profits:				
Meat animals	.024	4.70	2.26	28.16[b]
Grains and forage	.013	2.55		
Other	.033	6.47	3.10	38.63[b]

[a] In perpetuity at 5 percent.
[b] Twenty years at 5 percent.

stock group since it includes only meat processing as a sector producing for final demand. This grouping facilitates illustration of certain aspects of the theoretical discussion of chapter VII. It will be assumed, as was discussed earlier, that withdrawals of water from feed and forage crops will impose a cost externality on feeding and meat processing, so as to force these activities to phase out. This assumption is implicit in the derivation of the income estimates and the construction of figure 11. In order to illustrate possible magnitudes of the capitalized value of water use in this industry group, it will be necessary to make assumptions about land, capital, and labor mobilities. We wish to emphasize the illustrative nature of these assumptions, since they are not based on an empirical study. Three sets of assumptions will be used to identify income externalities and the resulting capitalized value estimates.

The simplest assumption with regard to rent and land use is that land has no alternative use. Two major considerations influence the possibility of alternative uses of land: dryland farming and urban use. Dryland farming in an arid area is patently unfeasible; so we dispense with that possibility. The possibility of urban use is a potential for any area, particularly in southern California. However, if this eventually were imminent the desirability of transferring irrigation water from the area would be questionable and would alter the speculative value of the water. We, therefore, assume no alternative use for land and proceed to estimate a capital value for the land-water complex based on a rental, income flow concept.

Obviously the choice of discount rate and the time period of capitalization affects the value estimate. Since we have not done a systematic study of this problem and since our presentation here is only meant to be illustrative, the variables are chosen somewhat arbitrarily and without justification. The present value of an income flow of rent per acre-foot from table 19, which is $6.27 per year in perpetuity at a 5 percent discount rate, is $125.40; discounted for 50 years, it is approximately $114.49.

With regard to capital facilities and equipment mobility, it will be assumed that only the in-place facilities (buildings, feedlot pens, etc.) are immobile. It will be assumed that either the "rolling stock" (tractors, trucks, crop equipment, etc.) is mobile or that the rate of water withdrawal allows full depreciation. The rate of technological obsolescence in the meat-packing industry is considered high, so it is not unreasonable to suppose that either depreciation or obsolescence would reduce these capital losses to a minimum especially if water supply were withdrawn over a 30-year period, as was suggested above. An examination of types of capital equipment used in feed and forage production and livestock feeding from a study in the Imperial Valley indicates that 48 percent of total investment is in nonmovable facilities and 52 percent is rolling stock.[11] Estimates for the meat-packing industry are that 75 percent of investment is movable and subject to obsolescence or short-lived depreciation.[12] Referring to table 19, it will be noted that $0.128 of capital return for meat processing is direct and $0.070 is indirect; the indirect is derived from $0.024 from the meat animal sector, $0.013 from grains and forage, and $0.033 from all other sectors. These coefficients are converted to a per-acre-foot basis by dividing by the water multiplier of meat processing for grains and forage crops. Assuming 25 percent unrecoverable capital income for meat processing and 48 percent for the others yields the next column in the table. Assuming 20 years of productive life remaining in these facilities at the time of their abandonment and a 5 percent discount rate, we calculate the present value of these income flows as found in the last column.

The remaining income category is wages and salaries, constituting the largest income share. One would suppose most labor to be fairly mobile in this area since it is close to a metropolitan center and engaged in commercial agricultural enterprise and agriculture-related sectors. The only assumption which seems reasonable without a detailed survey is that labor movement and reemployment has a cost, but that all labor is mobile. To illustrate a cost of movement, one could assume some

[11] H. O. Carter, G. W. Dean and P. H. Maxwell, *Economics of Cattle Feeding on Imperial Valley Field Crop Farms,* California Agricultural Experiment Station Bulletin 813, 1964. We arrived at these percentages by classifying the investments in table 13, page 27, of the bulletin.

[12] Personal conversation with meat packing plant management.

percentage of income loss. For example, one-half a year's wages lost as a cost of movement and retraining adds $23.43 per acre-foot as a cost of transfer; i.e., one-half of the wage payment per acre-foot in table 19. According to the above assumptions, the components of losses related to water withdrawal are: $125.40 for land and water, $146.53 ($79.74 + 28.16 + 38.63) for immobile capital facilities and $23.43 (ad hoc estimate not shown in table 19) as a cost of labor movement. These add to a total of $295.36 per acre-foot.

It was pointed out in the first part of chapter VII that analysis and estimates of income externalities could be used for several purposes: (1) to assess the efficiency of market transfers, (2) to specify conditions for national-income-increasing transfers, (3) to serve as alternative cost guidelines for regions contemplating developing outside sources of supply, and (4) to identify the economic interests affecting political decisions on water use. Uses of the estimates for (1), (2) and (3) are all related. According to the preceding illustrative estimates, market transactions in water rights would likely take place in the feed and forage sector at a price equal to the present value of the rental income flow (the return to land and fixed capital), $125.40 per acre-foot. This assumes that owners of water rights are also the owners of the land and associated fixed capital facilities and that they would charge a price sufficient to compensate for their capital losses. This kind of a transaction would impose externalities of $107.90 ($79.74 + 28.16) per acre-foot on owners of capital in meat processing and the feeding of meat animals; $38.63 to owners of capital in other sectors; and $23.43 per acre-foot in moving costs on wage and salaried employees. If the marginal social value in the buying use were just equal to the price necessary to induce sale (the value from rental and capital income for the sellers in the feed and forage sector), then national income would be reduced by $169.96 per acre-foot.

According to the classification scheme of chapter VII, the income effects imposed on meat processing and feeding sectors would be forward-linked [type (3) effects] and could induce a market response from these processing sectors. The response would be in the form of a price increase to grain and forage producers to maintain current levels of output. The amount of the price increase would be limited to bidding away returns to fixed plant and location rent. Thus, for the above example, it would be possible for the $107.90 to be transferred back to grain and forage producers, resulting in an increase in the price of water by that amount. If this mechanism were operative then the water price would rise from $125.40 to $233.30 (125.40 + 107.90) and the amount of the externality would be reduced to $38.63 capital loss for other sectors and

$23.43 loss from cost of labor movement. The $38.60 represents a type (2) externality, i.e., from the selling of inputs.

An estimate for a national-income-increasing transfer, using the above assumptions, is that the capitalized value of water in the new use— municipal use in Los Angeles County, for example—must be at least equal to the total capitalized income loss of $295 per acre-foot presented above. All of the income externalities which can be theoretically specified are not included in the above estimate. Household income consumption effects are not included, and, as was discussed in chapter VII, externalities in the public sector, loss of investment in houses, scale economies, and so forth are relevant although difficult to measure.

CONCLUSIONS

Normative aspects of the income externality pertain to both income distributional effects and effects on national income (efficiency). Our concern has been with the efficiency considerations, which is not to imply that the equity considerations are not important. Normative efficiency conditions are objectively specifiable and are at least conceptually determinable. We make no claim to being exempt from bias. However, an attempt has been made to point out assumptions as explicitly as possible, so that the analysis and presentation of data in this chapter and the conceptual analysis of the previous one are amenable to reinterpretation under different sets of conditions. It is obvious that our estimates of income externalities for water withdrawals from agriculture are sensitive to the assumptions from which they were derived.

It is quite obvious that *the critical assumptions concern the amount of immobility in capital, land, and labor resources.* The amount of immobility and the consequent externality income effect are dependent upon the timing of withdrawals. This reflects the same problem that national agriculture has experienced over the past several decades. Federal programs have been partially oriented toward slowing down the rate of resource transfer.

The order of magnitude of the above estimates calls into question the desirability of large block withdrawals of water from developed agricultural areas, as some have proposed.[13] It seems doubtful that any manipulation of data or assumptions would radically alter the order of magnitude of the above estimates. The immobility assumptions may be conservative for some rate of withdrawal and liberal for other rates. That is a question to be answered by more detailed study.

---

[13] See, for example, Jack Hirshleifer, James C. DeHaven, and Jerome W. Milliman, *Water Supply* (University of Chicago Press, 1960).

APPENDIX TABLES FOR CHAPTER VIII

TABLE A-VIII-1. TECHNICAL COEFFICIENTS, CALIFORNIA ECONOMY, 1954a

Sector Numbers	1 Meat animals	2 Poultry and eggs	3 Farm dairy prod.	4 Grains	5 Cotton	6 Veg.	7 Fruits and nuts	8 Citrus	9 Forage	10 Misc. agri.	11 Grain mill prod.	12 Meat and poultry proc.
1 Meat animals and products	—	—	—	—	—	—	—	—	—	—	—	.306770
2 Poultry and eggs	—	.183728	—	—	—	—	—	—	—	—	—	.061247
3 Farm dairy products	—	—	.027144	—	—	—	—	—	—	—	—	—
4 Food and feed grains	.042727	.070204	.022419	.042578	—	—	—	—	—	.001187	.285401	—
5 Cotton	—	—	—	—	.003812	—	—	—	—	—	—	—
6 Vegetables	—	—	—	—	—	.011401	—	—	—	—	—	—
7 Fruit (excluding citrus) and nuts	—	—	—	—	—	—	—	—	—	—	—	—
8 Citrus	—	—	—	—	—	—	—	.000015	—	—	—	—
9 Forage	.266292	—	.232466	—	—	—	—	—	—	.023475	.016676	—
10 Miscellaneous agriculture	.000318	—	—	.041011	.101780	.033220	.039041	.025595	.057344	.027414	.061989	.000244
11 Grain mill products	—	—	.005752	—	—	—	—	—	—	.000421	—	—
12 Meat and poultry processing	.046500	.343149	.090181	—	—	—	—	—	—	—	.002373	.000828
13 Dairy products	—	—	—	—	—	—	—	—	—	.001425	.005001	.041712
14 Canning, preserving, freezing	—	—	—	—	—	—	—	—	—	—	.002643	.002160
15 Miscellaneous agri. processing	—	—	—	—	—	—	—	—	—	.003392	.031261	.004972

16 Chemicals and fertilizers	.002692	.003251	.003266	.039053	.030897	.016663	.036382	.021012	.023995	.015971	.009121	.003834
17 Petroleum	.002538	.003827	.003664	.020513	.007259	.008228	.028654	.014246	.016848	.029066	.001538	.000959
18 Fabricated metals and machinery	.003176	.005487	.011309	.048389	.014476	.017534	.040301	.027507	.050363	.045868	.007835	.007667
19 Aircraft and parts	—	—	—	—	—	—	—	—	—	—	—	—
20 Primary metals	—	—	—	—	—	—	—	—	—	—	—	—
21 Other manufacturing	.001680	.022026	.003534	.002938	.002504	.040169	.021440	.044527	.002621	.009770	.028271	.005523
22 Mining	—	—	—	.000106	.000214	.000156	.000483	.000277	.000315	.000092	.000139	—
23 Utilities	.004257	.005256	.004072	.002776	.002775	.002611	.008744	.005116	.001622	.010364	.005286	.003337
24 Selected services	.002434	.005320	.003830	.019911	.006601	.007932	.026354	.014546	.019602	.020120	.002814	.002209
25 Trade and transportation	.047477	.097282	.043107	.078446	.044318	.046167	.053459	.050665	.063349	.052446	.069203	.026018
26 Unallocated	.007578	.016872	.021156	.008522	.007945	.005678	.017415	.017779	.012704	.013522	.018801	.005219
27 Scrap and byproducts	.027345	.003001	.018190	—	—	—	—	—	—	.001011	.097286	.043811
28 Net imports	.353739	.072363	.055503	.068462	.033015	.032486	.053865	.035455	.050275	.060401	.092834	.260102
29 Maintenance construction	.011179	.007117	.012051	.013352	.012187	.008320	.007891	.007773	.009459	.011046	.001303	.001913
30 New construction	—	—	—	—	—	—	—	—	—	—	—	—
31 State and local governments	.016822	.014931	.031029	.039241	.022987	.020076	.034071	.034295	.055843	.029622	.003091	.001884
32 Federal government	.000796	.002610	.001624	.005239	.004963	.004446	.005809	.005488	.006495	.007592	.020263	.009400
37 Households	.162449	.143573	.409701	.569461	.704265	.744910	.626089	.695702	.629162	.635794	.236870	.210190

TABLE A-VIII-1. (Continued)

13 Dairy prod.	14 Canning, preserv., freeze.	15 Misc. agri. proc.	16 Chem. and fert.	17 Petro-leum	18 Fab. metals and mach.	19 Air-craft	20 Primary metals	21 Other mfg.	22 Mining	23 Utili-ties	24 Selected services	25 Trade and trans.	26 Unal-located	Sector Numbers
.000056	—	—	—	—	—	—	—	.000006	—	—	—	—	—	1
.485115	.000005	.001537	—	—	—	—	—	—	—	—	—	—	—	2
—	—	.001889	.000113	—	—	—	—	—	—	—	—	—	—	3
—	—	—	—	—	—	—	—	—	—	—	—	—	—	4
—	.126612	.004478	—	—	—	—	—	.000242	—	—	—	—	—	5
—	—	—	—	—	—	—	—	—	—	—	—	—	—	6
—	.170156	.026277	.000208	—	—	—	—	—	—	—	—	—	—	7
—	.011004	—	—	—	—	—	—	—	—	—	—	—	—	8
—	—	—	—	—	—	—	—	—	—	—	—	—	—	9
—	.055737	.028151	.005472	—	—	—	.00160	.000642	—	—	—	—	—	10
.000314	.006956	.048477	.002443	—	.000001	—	—	—	—	.000003	.002342	.000067	.000094	11
.002855	.011816	.012962	.019329	.000002	—	—	—	.000420	—	.000363	.017447	.000211	.001437	12
.083683	.000758	.007852	.000634	—	—	—	—	.000080	—	.000224	.013689	.000486	.000526	13
.001777	.016059	.006516	.001077	—	—	—	—	—	—	.000165	.010443	.000086	.000412	14
.038640	.078311	.180216	.017434	.000001	.000003	—	.000006	.000364	—	.000406	.042309	.002643	.001072	15

.003717	.011542	.031955	.197307	.011020	.009059	.004506	.003574	.019827	.026454	.000535	.005973	.001791	.003349			16
.002308	.001134	.002721	.023448	.372234	.002406	.003828	.020220	.006056	.021574	.050450	.005598	.015872	.013280			17
.014165	.069801	.012638	.013487	.010872	.199224	.090750	.009533	.024205	.024560	.007909	.046313	.009817	.001038			18
–	–	–	–	–	.000667	.091473	–	–	–	–	.000178	.000701	–			19
–	–	.031374	.008641	.000271	.077920	.035650	.204746	.007513	.009882	.000730	.000043	.001446	.000263			20
.017155	.048601	.000129	.031189	.006664	.047572	.040515	.012903	.181808	.025670	.005430	.024067	.021218	.049341			21
–	–	.009481	.013286	.000683	.000267	–	.025130	.006097	.014066	–	–	.000052	–			22
.007846	.005826	.009070	.014392	.007621	.008035	.011160	.016639	.013382	.037411	.123293	.024370	.021245	.053484			23
.006521	.007410	–	.003179	.003362	.003107	.003613	.002512	.005111	.025808	.005451	.041301	.024693	.009129			24
.034767	.027445	.043357	.039694	.040378	.035189	.021441	.045967	.044151	.026366	.020939	.057869	.035376	.032990			25
.010674	.032835	.033240	.039341	.013709	.013820	.015587	.009101	.018483	.020679	.018022	.068852	.090243	.066028			26
–	–	–	.045997	.000003	.000868	–	.002790	–	–	.000526	–	–	–			27
.035738	.066258	.147203	.198791	.014501	.178915	.102988	.150985	.048319	.018332	.044289	.024028	.022469			28
.003792	.003571	.002963	.001658	.001542	.002598	.003859	.004369	.002694	.001617	.056653	.005386	.024919	.073792			29
–	–	–	–	–	–	–	–	–	–	–	–	–	–			30
.007160	.007463	.008221	.006744	.022602	.005931	.003340	.006023	.006933	.064712	.100342	.030496	.041875	.097408			31
.022077	.037724	.043033	.048820	.052245	.047608	.023869	.039406	.051198	.041413	.069705	.054796	.068069	.022433			32
.221640	.202974	.306260	.267313	.442290	.366806	.547420	.260609	.457009	.611465	.520518	.504236	.615160	.551452			37

a Each entry shows dollars of direct purchases from the California sector listed at the left by the California sector listed at the top per dollar of output of the latter sector.

Source: William E. Martin and Harold O. Carter, *A California Interindustry Analysis Emphasizing Agriculture*, Giannini Foundation Research Report No. 250, University of California, Berkeley, Agriculture Experiment Station, 1962, app. A, table II-1.

TABLE A-VIII-2. INTERDEPENDENCY COEFFICIENTS, CALIFORNIA ECONOMY, 1954[a]

Sector Numbers		1 Meat animals	2 Poultry and eggs	3 Farm dairy prod.	4 Grains	5 Cotton	6 Veg.	7 Fruits and nuts	8 Citrus	9 Forage	10 Misc. agri.	11 Grain mill prod.	12 Meat and poultry proc.
1	Meat animals and products	1.000296	.001132	.000408	.000541	.000399	.000256	.000543	.000339	.000406	.000812	.002241	.320397
2	Poultry and eggs	.000079	1.225396	.000110	.000138	.000102	.000066	.000139	.000087	.000104	.000211	.000630	.078383
3	Farm dairy products	.000209	.000893	1.028198	.000265	.000132	.000124	.000299	.000188	.000238	.000254	.001742	.000668
4	Food and feed grains	.059559	.224002	.053743	1.044731	.000281	.000140	.000257	.000161	.000235	.001671	.318960	.033645
5	Cotton	.000003	.000015	.000004	.000004	1.003829	.000014	.000009	.000015	.000003	.000005	.000012	.000004
6	Vegetables	.000057	.000298	.000088	.000064	.000036	1.011562	.000071	.000043	.000055	.000076	.000633	.000376
7	Fruit (excluding citrus) and nuts	.000147	.000801	.000230	.000160	.000101	.000075	1.000170	.000105	.000133	.000237	.001725	.000693
8	Citrus	.000004	.000018	.000005	.000004	.000002	.000002	.000005	1.000018	.000004	.000004	.000038	.000029
9	Forage	.267695	.008261	.241323	.001260	.002621	.000919	.001177	.000765	1.001564	.024474	.019212	.086401
10	Miscellaneous agriculture	.018849	.010832	.022883	.044568	.105542	.034843	.040655	.026661	.059364	1.030073	.016355	.007169
11	Grain mill products	.049904	.449597	.099296	.000507	.000377	.000242	.000513	.000319	.000404	.001076	1.069006	.045466

12	Meat and poultry processing	.000967	.003688	.001331	.001764	.001299	.000835	.001770	.001103	.001324	.002647	.007303	1.044420
13	Dairy products	.000419	.001791	.000596	.000531	.000265	.000248	.000599	.000377	.000478	.000510	.003493	.001339
14	Canning, preserving, freezing	.000329	.001629	.000500	.000387	.000200	.000173	.000439	.000267	.060341	.000365	.003409	.002605
15	Miscellaneous agri. processing	.003344	.019719	.005386	.003151	.002195	.001523	.003236	.002041	.002610	.006458	.043316	.009406
16	Chemicals and fertilizers	.016642	.025493	.017499	.054314	.042162	.024097	.049314	.029745	.033449	.024170	.033097	.012921
17	Petroleum	.018734	.026503	.020752	.043183	.021217	.019151	.054491	.029483	.035097	.054089	.021989	.011322
18	Fabricated metals and machinery	.028901	.034557	.038564	.070897	.022347	.028171	.058633	.040948	.070639	.065279	.038135	.023040
19	Aircraft and parts	.000087	.000173	.000094	.000133	.000067	.000067	.000103	.000083	.000117	.000105	.000121	.000072
20	Primary metals	.003308	.004664	.004327	.007924	.003385	.003689	.006836	.005097	.007613	.007054	.004840	.002722
21	Other manufacturing	.011816	.062779	.017616	.016186	.011013	.055834	.037673	.062897	.014389	.022330	.050364	.017873
22	Mining	.000508	.000982	.000584	.001206	.000977	.000952	.001624	.001239	.001107	.000808	.001112	.000412
23	Utilities	.010895	.021814	.012385	.010985	.008792	.007936	.017725	.012368	.008783	.018340	.016126	.010877
24	Selected services	.012532	.019561	.013933	.026256	.011350	.011398	.031455	.018509	.024691	.025006	.015166	.008862
25	Trade and transportation	.081552	.186595	.081422	.098287	.058128	.057520	.070021	.063791	.078373	.068172	.116494	.068859
26	Unallocated	.024425	.057526	.040778	.026405	.019607	.016175	.033449	.030925	.027541	.027660	.042813	.021784

TABLE A-VIII-2. (Continued)

13	14	15	16	17	18	19	20	21	22	23	24	25	26	Sector Numbers
Dairy prod.	Canning, preserv., freeze.	Misc. agri. proc.	Chem. and fert.	Petro-leum	Fab. metals and mach.	Air-craft	Primary metals	Other mfg.	Mining	Utili-ties	Selected services	Trade and trans.	Unal-located	
.001579	.004708	.005750	.007974	.000222	.000183	.000131	.000117	.000456	.000433	.000220	.006308	.000345	.000645	1
.000566	.001347	.003716	.002003	.000057	.000047	.000033	.000030	.000114	.000111	.000056	.001651	.000094	.000163	2
.544679	.011080	.055535	.000677	.000107	.000092	.000080	.000086	.000173	.000274	.000224	.008134	.000552	.000440	3
.029695	.004729	.022765	.002509	.000081	.000072	.000051	.000111	.000133	.000164	.000069	.002922	.000211	.000186	4
.000010	.000022	.000015	.000014	.000005	.000019	.000016	.000006	.000299	.000010	.000003	.000012	.000009	.000017	5
.000602	.130749	.006663	.000352	.000024	.000020	.000017	.000018	.000032	.000063	.000045	.001752	.000087	.000092	6
.001931	.175754	.033711	.001296	.000063	.000052	.000041	.000042	.000090	.000144	.000086	.003488	.000223	.000176	7
.000030	.011195	.000095	.000019	.000002	.000001	.000001	.000001	.000002	.000004	.000003	.000128	.000005	.000007	8
.128303	.003465	.004837	.002575	.000092	.000078	.000059	.000059	.000193	.000194	.000115	.003765	.000236	.000287	9
.014034	.073702	.039219	.008321	.000202	.000201	.000140	.000108	.001115	.000358	.000094	.003031	.000271	.000235	10
.056022	.013759	.065856	.005961	.000198	.000182	.000127	.000331	.000305	.000404	.000157	.007418	.000551	.000432	11

	13	14	15	16	17	18	19	20	21	22	23	24	25	26
12	.005145	.015346	.018741	0.25991	.000724	.000594	.000425	.000381	.001462	.001409	.000715	.020561	.001122	.002102
13	1.092306	.002167	.011100	.001358	.000215	.000185	.000160	.000173	.000347	.000549	.000448	.016312	.001107	.000882
14	.002736	1.017351	.008649	.001759	.000147	.000122	.000106	.000108	.000176	.000402	.000306	.011663	.000492	.000631
15	.055628	.100393	1.226471	.028039	.001252	.001039	.000782	.000843	.002027	.002603	.001250	.057106	.005260	.002545
16	.018160	.036238	.056421	1.251292	.023227	.017398	.010131	.008558	.031979	.036186	.002854	.013914	.004865	.007114
17	.019195	.024079	.018351	.054917	1.598426	.014095	.013606	.046986	.018500	.043325	.093844	.018985	.032527	.030702
18	.043740	.113723	.032562	.027872	.024456	1.254808	.129074	.019167	.040225	.036666	.014020	.067607	.016981	.006188
19	.000105	.000143	.000089	.000073	.000075	.000968	1.100808	.000067	.000080	.000063	.000036	.000316	.000826	.000041
20	.005074	.012611	.004613	.017292	.003564	.124123	.062863	1.260258	.016181	.017133	.002674	.007521	.004087	.001850
21	.039410	.092138	.062846	.058507	.019763	.079548	.066603	.026268	1.230733	.040400	.012168	.047431	.036477	.068222
22	.000709	.001564	.001487	.017721	.001644	.004243	.002197	.032441	.008482	1.015483	.000253	.000721	.000479	.000591
23	.020723	.020649	.023518	.029692	.018972	.019081	.020586	.029629	.024455	.049444	1.144588	.039723	.033912	.068895
24	.017303	.020401	.017926	.008476	.008230	.006962	.006607	.006701	.009299	.029658	.008081	1.048039	.028674	.012422
25	.090504	.071782	.079496	.066195	.072073	.058729	.038148	.067093	.063472	.039370	.031694	.079619	1.047306	.044577
26	.043298	.059640	.061170	.064901	.033274	.029018	.027503	.022454	.034337	.033252	.027803	.091977	.105947	1.079646

a Each entry shows dollars of direct and indirect requirements for products of the California sector listed at the left per dollar of final demand for products of the California sector listed at the top.

Source: William E. Martin and Harold O. Carter, *A California Interindustry Analysis Emphasizing Agriculture*, Giannini Foundation Research Report No. 250, University of California, Berkeley, Agricultural Experiment Station, 1962, app. A, table II-1.

TABLE A-VIII-3. INCOME AND WATER COEFFICIENTS BY ECONOMIC SECTORS, CALIFORNIA ECONOMY, 1954

	1 Meat animals	2 Poultry and eggs	3 Farm dairy prod.	4 Grains	5 Cotton	6 Veg.	7 Fruits and nuts	8 Citrus	9 Forage	10 Misc. agri.	11 Grain mill prod.	12 Meat and poultry proc.	13 Dairy prod.
Wages	.087	.153	.283	.161	.245	.324	.493	.342	.306	.539	.086	.082	.161
Rent				.25	.20	.09	.09	.09	.25	.25			
Profits	.075	.009	.126	.158	.259	.331	.043	.261	.073	—	.151	.128	.061
Water (Acre-ft/$1,000)				23.8	8.4	3.2	7.7	3.2	46.7	3.94			

	14 Canning, preserv., freeze.	15 Misc. agri. proc.	16 Chem. and fert.	17 Petroleum	18 Fab. metals and mach.	19 Aircraft	20 Primary metals	21 Other mfg.	22 Mining	23 Utilities	24 Selected services	25 Trade and trans.	26 Unallocated
Wages	.127	.146	.220	.101	.301	.281	.213	.308	.163	.368	.279	.597	.321
Rent													
Profits	.076	.160	.047	.341	.066	.266	.048	.149	.498	.152	.225	.018	.230
Water (Acre-ft/$1,000)													

Sources: Pinhas Zusman and Irving Hoch, *Resource and Capital Requirement Matrices for the California Economy*, Giannini Foundation Research Report No. 284, University of California, Berkeley, Agricultural Experiment Station, 1965, p. 24, table 6; and *Guide Lines to Production Costs and Practices, Imperial County Crops*, University of California Agricultural Extension Service, Circular 104. For methodology, see text.

CHAPTER IX

CONCLUSIONS

The features of water as an economic resource which gave rise to economic conditions meriting special study are the random elements in its supply and the complexity of the systems, natural and manmade, through which it flows. The regulation and development of water use have stimulated the formation of unique institutions, legal and organizational, to handle the problems of supply development, allocation, and reallocation. This study has provided an analysis of some important examples of these institutions in terms of the ways in which they facilitate or obstruct economically efficient transfers among uses. The primary aspect of the transfer process studied here is the occurrence of external effects which result from private transactions. When points of diversion or uses are changed, the physical supply of water to third parties (other than buyer and seller) is sometimes affected. Laws designed to protect the third parties, while desirable from an equity point of view, are frequently inefficiently defined from an economic viewpoint and have the tendency of immobilizing the resource. The same can be true of the rules adopted by organizations.

Changing uses and points of diversion may affect not only direct water users but also the incomes of economic sectors linked by exchange with water-using firms. Such effects tend to immobilize the resource at the political level of decision-making. Analyses of these two types of externalities and their implications for the functioning of the legal system and the design of water management institutions have been the subjects of the present study.

PHYSICAL EXTERNALITIES AND THE LAW

Much of the alleged inefficiency engendered by water law stems from the inherent uncertainties or randomness of water flows themselves, further uncertainties due to a lack of knowledge concerning the mechanics of water systems (return flow phenomena, etc.), and the resultant variations which occur in the testimony of experts and the judgments of courts. The present study has suggested that administrative procedures for implementing the law are superior to court procedures. This conclusion is based primarily on the more advantageous use and availability of impartial engineering data. In transfer cases handled by both the court procedure in Colorado and the administrative procedure in New Mexico, it is apparent that neither buyer nor seller knows exactly what the right being negotiated involves in terms of the quantity which can be diverted. This uncertainty relates to the amount historically diverted, the amount "beneficially" used, and the effect of the proposed transfer on supplies to other users.

The first uncertainty can be reduced by adjudication proceedings, which in effect quantify established rights. Programs of continuing adjudication of rights and the development of hydrologic stream-flow models to study the physical interrelatedness of water users constitute a big step in the modernization of procedures for rational water transfer. Analogue and digital computer models have been developed for selected streams in Colorado and other states by university researchers, the U.S. Geological Survey, and the Bureau of Reclamation. These models are designed to estimate the effects of changing uses and places of use on the river regime. Continued efforts to improve these models so that they become practical and reliable information sources for decisions on water transfers are of vital importance. Certainly the processes of law can never be any more rational in adjusting existing water supplies to the requirements of a developing society than is permitted by the information sources upon which legal decisions are based.

It was pointed out in chapter III that present laws do not recognize return flows as the property of the water user who generates them. Thus existing return flows are protected, but new return flows which would be created by a water transfer never get valued since they cannot be sold to the new recipients. A process analogous to the sale of return flows would improve the efficiency of transfers.

ORGANIZATIONS

Judging the efficacy of legal systems for water allocation depends upon several factors. Protection of property rights is one of the foundations of Western society. Laws and legal procedures have served admirably as a basic framework of order for mobilizing the energies and resources of the United States for economic growth. However, the law is only a framework. The mutual ditch company and various kinds of water districts serve as organizations for allocating water within the broad framework of law. As the pressure of growing water demands presses against fixed supplies, it becomes imperative that these organizations perform their allocative functions more efficiently and that the law permit them to do so.

Different types of water management organizations have different legal and geographical scopes. Thus the degree to which they internalize all impacts of their own decisions will differ. For example, the mutual ditch company usually has only one diversion point and return flow interdependencies are minimal, so that intracompany water exchanges are not hampered by return flow phenomena. The company affords a market framework for members' private interests to decide upon water rentals and sales. Where physical interdependencies among members do occur, the company has rules for deciding compensation to disadvantaged members. The fact that a company is composed of individuals with a common purpose and with common values concerning the function of the organization makes the system readily capable of rule enforcement and rule change. The companies' organizational rules govern a narrow and homogeneous set of behavior patterns, and thus are not as difficult to change and enforce as court law. Therein lies much of the superiority of specialized organizations for dealing with the allocation of a complex resource like water.

The existence of two relatively new districts in Colorado, each having different rules affecting the internal reallocation of water, suggests that organizations with desirable economic features do not spontaneously come into existence. The contrast between the two districts in terms of the effect of their operating rules on efficiency points up the need for informed guidance in district formation; i.e., in institutional design. How readily the districts' rules change and adapt to economic and social forces after initial formation is a question of considerable importance, since census data indicate that this is the most important organization in terms of total water use.

The district form of organization, somewhat imperfectly, internalizes income externalities by taxing indirect beneficiaries and by allowing them some control in district affairs. The northern Colorado district discussed above is governed by an appointed board of directors; so the users have only indirect influence on district affairs. This district is forbidden by statute to sell water outside its boundaries. Sales of water to parties outside the district have apparently occurred only in California.

As suggested earlier in the book, the formation of private organizations such as the mutual ditch company and public organizations such as the conservancy district stemmed originally from a financial need. The function of reallocation or providing a vehicle for transfers of water to new uses was somewhat incidental. The economic pressure for providing such functions is only now being experienced as water becomes relatively scarcer. It is fallacious to think that social forces automatically bring into existence appropriate institutions. One might conclude that where a change in law or organization operating rules is possible by which all parties could be made better off, the failure of such a change to take place must be attributable to a lack of information or a lack of an appropriate communication and control structure for changing rules. However, in situations where some people are made better off and some worse off from a rule change, the change may not take place because of uncertainties in predicting consequences and also because there is no procedure for compensating the losers. In situations where incommensurable variables are involved in a change—e.g., income and the psychic cost of changing habitual behavior—it is impossible for an outside observer to measure on an a priori basis whether the change is desirable or not. The best that can be done is to identify whether the existing communication and control structure is appropriate for efficient decisions.

In situations where there has been little growth and the laws and organizational systems have been fairly stable, it appears that water users view changes in the system as a zero-sum game; i.e., the efforts of some users to change the rules of the game are viewed as a strategy to gain an advantage which invariably must be a loss to someone else. Litigation over the rules then becomes essentially a power struggle with the "spoils" often going to the side with the cleverest legal counsel. In areas where rapid growth is taking place it appears that water users perceive the situation as a non-zero-sum game and look upon organizational and legal innovations as opportunities for improving everyone's welfare.

THE INCOME EXTERNALITY

Broadly conceived, the efficiency criterion for water transfers should be conceptualized in the same benefit-cost framework of analysis as public investment projects. In this context the economic aspects of a transfer are evaluated in terms of national income *before and after* the transfer. The income *externality* is defined as that part of the change in national income, either positive or negative, occurring as a result of the transfer but not considered in the calculations of the buyer or seller. The external income effects related to the buying use are essentially the same as the so-called secondary benefits of investment projects and, if existing at all, must stem from the existence of economies of scale or unused plant capacity and labor unemployment in sectors market-related to the buying use. The income externality at the seller's end, if any, occurs either from losing the advantages of economies of scale in private production and provision of public services or from factor immobilities. Externality effects may be partially analyzed through the use of regional input-output models. The problem does not appear to be amenable to completely general conclusions concerning the efficacy of present market solutions. The efficiency aspects of a market solution depend upon the rate of transfer, the type of use, and the structure of the regional economy. These are empirical questions, explicable only in the context of specific situations.

The value of water in industrial and municipal uses is generally much greater than the value in agricultural uses.[1] It appears likely, therefore, that one need not be concerned that uncounted secondary benefits and costs will prevent economically desirable transfers from taking place when the difference in direct value is of the order of magnitude of a factor of ten or one hundred, as some of these comparisons suggest. The calculation of the externality income effects of transfers would be important only in those prospective transfers where marginal values in use were of the same order of magnitude or in those situations where transfers are being compared to other sources of supply in terms of cost. In assessing the future water needs of a municipality, for example, one might consider the alternatives of buying up agricultural water supplies, putting in a desalinization plant, or investing in transfer facilities to bring in more distant undeveloped supplies. Or one might be considering as alternative sources of supply two different agricultural areas. In these situations, the income externality could be a crucial deciding factor.

For irrigated agriculture, the less obvious potential income externalities stem from the forward-linked interdependency effect. The forward-linked sectors for agriculture are composed of processing firms which contribute more value added to the final goods, on the average, than do the primary sectors. Therefore, consideration of the existence of alternative sources of supply of raw material inputs to established processing firms is of critical importance in evaluating transfers from irrigation uses. We have made the case in presenting the empirical example in chapter VIII that the livestock processing industry locates near the production site of feed and forage because of transportation cost considerations. We conclude, therefore, that market forces would phase out this processing industry if withdrawal of water phased out their feed and forage supply. This type of effect may result in the capitalized value of the income

---

[1] See, for example, Robert A. Young and William E. Martin, "The Economics of Arizona's Water Problem," *Arizona Review,* March 1967.

externality being as great as the private selling price of the water. (See table 19, chapter VIII.)

In ranking the research needs related to income externalities, the location sensitivity of processing firms and the magnitude of capital and labor immobilities as a function of the rate of water withdrawal are of first priority. Errors in the data of the input-output model arising out of incorrect measurement and structural specification would result in only fractional estimation errors for the interdependency effects.[2] However, varying the assumptions about mobilities and forward-linkage effects can change the externality estimates by multiples.

Income effects are inherently a part of any economic change. Economic considerations direct one's attention to comparing the gains and the losses; political considerations, to whom gains and losses accrue. Our examination of the water transfer income externality does not imply that the public should seek to maintain the status quo of a given pattern of use, but it does imply the need for more comprehensive decision procedures and calculations than are currently involved in private market transactions or most public decisions.

[2] See Edward W. Lungren, "Data Errors in a Leontief Input-Output Model," student paper read at the Western Economics Association meeting in 1967, for a computer case study of multiplier errors related to original data errors. Copies of the paper may be obtained from the Department of Economics, Colorado State University, Fort Collins.

INDEX